spirit seeker

Communion With Those on the Other Side of the Veil

Richard Moschella

BEYOND THE FRAY
Publishing

BEYOND THE FRAY

Publishing

We all have the capacity to share spiritual teachings and will do it through our own filters. This is the beauty of being human. We are all having our own experience.

- Kyle Gray

"Now if it be true that the living come from the dead, then our souls must exist in the other world, for if not, how could they have been born again?".

- Socrates

preface

I have been researching the paranormal and metaphysical world for decades, I have met and worked with so many different researchers and light workers. When embarking on my journey in this field, I truly feel that the right people were put on my path along the way. I have had so many incredible opportunities to learn from and work with these individuals. They also shared with me the books that helped them on their journey. Today I try to consume a few books a month to always keep learning and feeding my soul. This book you're holding in your hands is a book that details more of my journey in communicating with spirit but also showing you the reader how spirit is all around us. We will discuss topics that will help you understand the communication process and talk about signs that could show up in our daily lives. I will also reveal compelling personal stories of encounters my family and I have had with spirit.

I will also discuss some casefiles from locations that I have investigated along with my group the New Jersey Paranormal Project and will give you a greater knowledge of how we investigate locations and make a connection with the spirits that reside there. This will be a compilation of some of the knowledge I have discovered on my journey and the evidence and interaction I have had with spirit, that has made me a firm believer in the continuity of life. I know we all are spirit seekers and spend our life trying to learn from the lessons that we are faced with each day on our earthly journey. If we open up to spirit communication we will begin to see that they are more than willing to communicate with us. This book is a labor of love and a compilation of many years researching and working intuitively with spirit. These stories you will read in the following chapters are all examples of spirit communication.

You will gain insight on paranormal investigations and the approach myself and my group implement when investigating and working with spirit. I will also go into detail on the process of Spirit Art, In my opinion the most important and evidential proof of afterlife communication. I will also cover my beliefs on the spirit communication process and so much more. It's important to never stop learning and feeding your soul, good luck on your journey. If you're reading this book you are already a spirit seeker!

We Are All Spirit Seekers

candle shoppe of spirits

THE CANDLE SHOPPE of the Poconos located in Swiftwater Pennsylvania, would be a location that would prove to be one of the most interesting locations I ever investigated. I first heard about the quaint candle shop from a co-worker some time ago and filed it away among the many conversations one has in this field of places you should investigate. In late 2021 my schedule allowed me to get a few investigations in before the year would come to a close. I immediately thought about that conversation I had with a co-worker and reached out to the candle shop. I reached out to the owner, Linda Schlier about my interest to investigate her location. In the coming weeks I had the opportunity to chat with Linda about the location and set a date for my investigation. The investigation would take place the day before Thanksgiving, I reached out to my team and made them aware that we would be able to investigate this location nestled in the pocono mountains.

I began to put together a historical record for the location, this includes property history and also profiles of the people from the properties history. When we ask questions to spirit during spirit radio sessions, I feel that we get to bring up factual events and dates that could work as a trigger question for response. This information is collected from ancestry sites, find a grave and other websites that offer historical and paranormal information. One of the most detailed paranormal reports is from a television show called The Haunted that aired in 2009 on Animal Planet. The episode is entitled The Lost Souls of the Asylum. The episode is split into two separate episodes and The Candle Shoppe is featured on the second part of the show. Linda and her husband Jim are featured in the episode and recount their experiences at the location.

In May, 1891, Doctor William Redwood Fisher moved to Swiftwater Pennsylvania, where entered a partnership with Doctor Richard Slee. Richard Slee first came to Monroe County in the early 1890s. He had contracted cholera and traveled to Swiftwater to recuperate and enjoy the "fresh air and invigorating waters." Richard Slee stayed at the Swiftwater Inn owned by Arthur and Ella Maginnis. While resting at the Swiftwater Inn, Slee met and fell in love with the owner's daughter, Ella. Richard and Ella were married in 1892. Arthur Maginnis died and Ella, along with her mother, inherited the Swiftwater Inn and the surrounding acreage. Slee now had the perfect location to build his laboratory. In 1897, Slee established his laboratory, Pocono Biological Laboratories.

The Fisher Family

The Candle Shoppe of the Poconos was the home and laboratory of Doctor William Redwood Fisher. It was built in 1897, when the town of Swiftwater was a budding scientific community. Doctor Fisher lived in this home with his family, and he also used it as his workplace. Dr. Fisher had a biological research laboratory in the basement of his home. Here, he performed research on primates, mainly spider monkeys, which allowed for the creation of Smallpox and Yellow Fever vaccines.

The episode is very revealing on the activity that is being reported by staff and some customers of the candle shoppe. The reports range from seeing shadow figures to small ghostly forms of what is described to be small animals scurrying across the floors. The phantom sounds of people talking to children laughing as if playing in another room. Talking with one of the candle shop's employees, Marlena spoke about some of her encounters with the spirits of the candle shop. She has encountered so much different activity from dicarnet voices speaking to hearing movement in the shop, when no one is present. She also reported hearing someone walk up behind her and felt a breeze sweep over her that soon dissipated. All these encounters with spirits at the shop, although frightening to the experincers, I must reiterate that nothing is malevolent, negative or looking to cause harm. So many of the spirits that I have encountered doing my work are just trying to make the presence known. They are attached to a location because it was a place in life that they have affection for. This candle shop once was a home for this doctor and his family, memories were made here and events that brought extreme happiness and unfortley sorrow transpired behind it's walls.

Marlena told us that some mediums that have entered the shop have picked up on the presence of a young boy. The boy was Doctor Fisher's young son John who drowned by accident in the creek behind the home. When my group New Jersey Paranormal Project and I receive this information from our clients, it's important to research the stories. I wanted to know if what these mediums are picking up on could be a young child of the Fisher family. Having the name John, I began a search through ancestry records and found that John Redwood Fisher was born in Hoboken, New Jersey in 1883. The record goes on to show that he was born to Dr. and Mrs. William R. Fisher. He went on to get married and served in the military, he had two children Sarah and James. He passed away in June of 1959 at the age of seventy five years old and is buried in Vermont. In trying to find a child of the Fisher's that could have died young, I did come across one interesting piece of information. Saint Paul's cemetery in Swiftwater has one grave belonging to the Fisher family that is listed as unknown. The gravestone is quite weathered and one could barely make out the inscription; it does in fact appear to be a gravestone of a young child. The date of the death that is listed is February 17th 1878, this date does not match the Fisher's moving into the town of Swiftwater in 1891 and building the home in 1897 that is now the candle shop.

This tragedy of a child drowning in water certainly could have happened at the location and the mediums that are picking up on this incident could very well be correct. The name beginning with "J" could have stood for junior or whatever the unknown name is of the Fisher child buried with his or her family in Swiftwater. Even getting the name John could be a connection to the deceased child making reference to being a part of the Fisher's children. There is so much symbolism and ways to interpret messages coming from the spirit world. In the end I know that John Redwood Fisher that was born in 1883 did not drown in the creek behind the home in Swiftwater but perhaps a younger child did. The further back you go into history the more the family stories seem to fade away, almost erasing them forever. That is why it's so important to collect evidence and do our best to tell the story of these locations and give spirit a voice. I took it upon myself to give a voice to this young spirit and help learn the correct information. It took about a month after the investigation, combing historical websites and ancestry information and then, one morning sitting in my office, the young boy's name appeared on my computer screen. The information simply said, William Redwood Fisher II, he was born June 17th, 1874 and passed on February 17th, 1878. He would be a junior and that could be the "J" name the mediums that have visited the shop could have been picking up on. All the weeks of researching had paid off and now spirit has helped correct the story being told. At times this is all the spirit wants, to be remembered and have their story told. Now knowing the name of the Fishers young child that passed away, I did an ancestry search and found out that he passed away in Hoboken, New Jersey and not in Pennsylvania. It seems that the plot thickens and could be an ongoing search for information. The further back you go into history, historical information gets harder to follow, especially when it's about orderney families living their lives. I am happy that I was able to find the child's name and at least contribute in correcting the story being told.

When I arrived at the location, I walked immediately to the back of the shop and to the creek. I felt that something was pulling me to that location for a reason, once Marlena told us that some mediums felt that a child drowned in the creek, it all made sense to why I was being pulled towards the water. I even noted the experience on the episode we filmed at the candle shop. Once after walking the location's grounds, we went inside and walked down the basement stairs to where Dr Fisher performed his research. As we walked through the basement, one could sense that you're not alone down here. The basement is full of display cases that feature the Swiftwater medical research for vaccines and medical experiments These tools are the actual instruments that went into finding cures to fight devestinging diseases. The candle shop also proudly displays documents and the work of Dr Fisher and Dr Slee, along with all the other minds that were on the forefront of vaccine research in the area.

Unknown Fisher Grave - Swiftwater
Pennsylvania

The basement of the candle shop also is a seasonal

haunted attraction, it offers all the scares and creatures that could be found in theme park attractions. When my team arrived to investate, I did not disclose the location and also had a haunted attraction. It was the team's first time investigating, alongside some very creepy life-like props. I felt that a good area in the basement to set up some of the equipment would be in front of the display of Dr William Redwood Fisher. The display features his personal research items that he personally used. I felt that these items had importance to the doctor and might still act as a trigger object during the investigation. Also in the display case was an embalming machine donated by the family of Charlie Adams. The Adams family were local undertakers and some of their items are also included in the display. There are so many items just in this one case that spirit could still hold an attachment to. These items were used regularly in life and encountered many different people, from the doctor to the undertaker. Just imagine the residual energy that these items could still be holding onto. The tools that Dr Fisher used daily in his laboratory to the embalming of bodies that Adams helped get ready for burial. This is a paranormal perfect storm for activity in a location.

I want to discuss first residual energy and how this kind of activity can be experienced at locations. Residual energy are moments captured in the fabric of time and also can be recorded in the spaces where events in life took place. The reports of residual encounters with spirit are as follows. The spirits seen appear to be like moving pictures and typically will be seen in the same spots, walking down the same hallway, appearing in the same window, doing the same motion over and over. They will be unaware of the living people around them. Residual encounters do not have any interaction between the spirit and the witnesses. It's like watching a scene or audio from a movie play out in front of you, no interaction between the spirit or the living happens. Residual spirit activity can also be heard, I have investigated cases where witnesses have reported hearing footsteps, talking and sobbing occurring at locations. They occur at times in the same place, same time and even in the same room. The activity reported does not show any signs of intelligence or communication with the living. Residual sounds can be as follows, footsteps, knocking and voices.

The Stone Tape theory is the speculation that ghosts and hauntings are analogous to tape recordings, and that mental impressions during emotional or traumatic events can be projected in the form of energy, "recorded" onto rocks and other items and "replayed" under certain conditions. In Monroe County, Pennsylvania where the candle shop is located, the ground contains Sedimentary rocks. They are the most common rocks at or near the surface in Pennsylvania, they mostly consist of sandstone, siltstone, shale, and some conglomerate. The geologic rock composition in the area can also help record the energy of spirit and help record it at locations. It can also help with supplying energy that spirit activity needs to manifest and boost the energy at the locations. Limestone is also known for having heightened properties to boost paranormal activity at locations. The relationship between limestone and quartz deposits seem to present a strong correlation in the likelihood of heightened spirit activity.

Display Case with Medical Instruments

From the foundation of the candle shop to the items being displayed in the cases throughout the attraction, spirit energy can be imprinted and left behind. These items can still hold the energy of their previous owner, it's almost like a fingerprint being left behind. These energy fingerprints that are left behind can last a very long time on objects and also can be felt by sensitive people in their presence. Have you ever held an item in your hand and got a feeling from the object? Possibly it felt good or possibly did not feel ok? Ever walked into an antique shop and felt overcome by emotions or held an item and felt emotionally affected by it? If you answered yes to these questions you're sensitive and could have been picking up on the item's energy. Psychometry is the ability to hold an object of unknown history and be able to tell it's story. The person holding the object is able to interpret the object's energy and perform a reading. When this occurs it's like watching a needle come down on a vinyl record and the item's history and previous owners comes to life. So being set up in the basement and surrounded by the fondation of the building and all the artifacts being displayed, I felt that we should have a very good chance at spirit communication.

We are here to tell your story

We began the basement investigation by stating our intentions. I feel that it's very important to let the spirits know who we are and why we are in their space. I also include that we come out of love and respect to them and that we are only there to help tell their story if they are willing to communicate. If they wish not to communicate that is fine with us, we just ask for the same respect back that we are showing them. I feel that intention is very important for success in communication with spirit and getting them to feel comfortable with the presence of strangers asking them questions and invading their space. At the start of the investigation I set up my GS2 Laser grid that detects movement, temperature fluctuations and could detect shapes moving in the grid it displays. This was set up in a walkway close to the Dr Fisher display case. The laser grid was projected onto this area of the basement and it began to detect disturbances in the grid. The GS2 laser also documented temperature changes, movement and direction changes happening in the area the grid was being projected in. Literally anything that passes in front of the laser with significant enough mass will cause a visual disturbance in the pattern and trigger visual displays on the device. You can see in the video that we filmed that the device captured warm and cold anomalies happening in the projected area. There was also a lot of movement happening in the projected grid, at one point I even stepped into the laser grid to show that it was working correctly. What could have the grid been picking up that was breaking the lasers and moving through the basement?

GS2 Laser Grid

I felt the strong presence of human and animal spirits in the basement. In my mind's eye, I could see a man in a white lab coat walking in the basement, deep in thought. After researching the photos for the case the man resembled Dr Richard Slee, I felt that he also is attached to this location. The other anomalies that broke the laser grind could certainly be animals that were used for the research, possibly spider monkeys that met an unfortunate end, all for the advancement of medical science. I was really impressed with how the laser grid performed at this investigation and really provided the team and the clients with amazing evidence of spirit. Another place that the laser grid showed a ton of movement was the monkey cages that are still intact in the basement. I was getting so much activity and movement, I had to immediately reach out to another researcher and get his opinion. I wanted to make sure that the laser that was being projected onto the medal cages was not picking up our heat signature and giving us a false reading of activity. He suggested I try a control experiment when I returned home and use an animal cage. If the same activity happens, then possibly the laser and medal of the cage is picking up on human heat and movement being close to the cage. It is so important to be skeptical in this field and have a prove it to me attitude, this is why as investigators we need to implement our devices and really study how they work in the field. Once we exhaust all other methods to try and explain what we captured then we can say that we feel what we experienced is paranormal in nature. The control cage test did not reveal the same results that occurred in the basement of the candle shop. The activity that the laser grid documented in the monkey cages was extremely different then what my experiment revealed. I can say without a doubt that the motion that the laser grid picked up in the cages was in my opinion paranormal in nature.

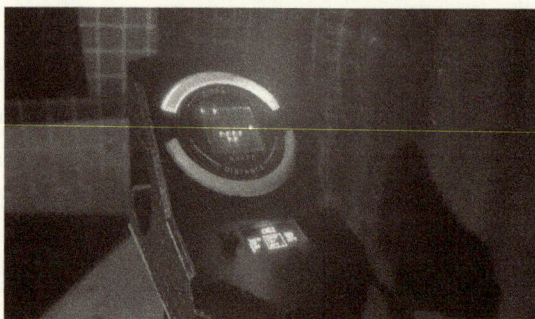

GS2 Laser Grid

When Marci Keck, one of the NJPP investigators implemented the technique of dowsing in the basement, the response from spirit she received was quite interesting. The use of dowsing rods goes back to 1518, when Martin Luther listed dowsing for metals as an act that broke the first commandment and was practicing occultism. There is more evidence that shows that this technique goes back into ancient times, dowsing or divining rods had been depicted in the artwork of ancient Egypt, China and Babylonia and that Queen Elizabeth I had employed dowsers to find metals to help make weapons. Dowsing is a type of divination used in attempts to locate ground water, buried metals or ores, gemstones, oil and even gravesites. It has even been used to locate missing people and yes have conversations with the dead. The idea that spirits can manipulate the rods and answer questions from the user is very intriguing. Spirit can use its energy to answer yes and no questions and also use the rods to guide the user to an area that spirit wants you to be aware of.

When our dowsing session began in the basement of the

candle shop, we started to communicate with spirits that were not the doctors and researchers. The spirits that started to communicate this time through the downing session were the children of the doctor and his wife Elizabeth, there was a dress that belonged to her being displayed in one of the display cases nearby. The beautiful white gown worn now by a mannequin let's visitors see through the ages, the clothing that Mrs Fisher wore in life. When Marci holding her dowsing rods asked if Mrs Fisher was present and the rods crossed for "Yes" one could not help but feel chills run up your spine. We also had a "Yes" response that one of Doctor Fisher's daughters was also in the basement with us. I personally feel that spirit can be wherever spirit wants to be and move throughout the location. I also believe that spirit is not stuck at a location either. If spirit is energy, spirit can be whenever it chooses be at any given time. If Doctor Fisher wanted to visit his childhood home in Mobile Alabama, he could do that. If perhaps he wanted to visit Hoboken, New Jersey and remember his time there, he can do that as well. There are no more physical laws that stop spirit from being where spirit wants to be. How fast can a thought happen in our minds? That is how fast spirits can travel, they are made up of beautiful energy and light.

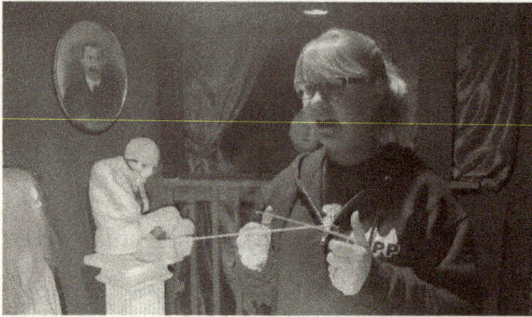

NJPP Investigator Marci Keck - Dowsing Rod
Session

There are even times where spirit has been in more than just one place at one time. A very good friend of mine told me a story about when he learned of his fathers passing. He told me that he was in his garage working on his car, when out of the blue, he heard his fathers voice in his head. His fathers voice was clear and deep, the message was "I love you". Besides hearing the voice of his father, he began to see images appear in his mind of the times his father would help him work on his cars. He waited a few minutes and called his brother to find out if he spoke with dad. Last year was tough on his father, he was diagnosed with late stage lung cancer and was nearing the end of his long fight. When his brother answered the phone he noticed his voice was nervous and was holding back tears.

His brother told him that he was in the yard working and out of the corner of his eye saw his father standing in the yard with him, he heard him say "I love you" and as he turned to see who was there, the image of his father was gone. The two brothers, states away from each other, both had an encounter with the spirit of their father at the same time. After sharing the experience with one another, they placed a call to the hospital where their father was being cared for and spoke to the nurse. The nurse was surprised to hear from the family so fast and asked if someone called them about their father, they both told her they had a feeling that something happened. The nurse got a doctor on the phone and that is when they both knew that their father lost his battle with this terrible disease. They both took comfort in knowing that dad was now freed from the illness that slowly took its toll on him. They both felt that their father came to them to let them know he was alright and still would always be around them. This is a great example of how spirit can be at two places at the same time and give you the reader an understanding at how spirit works in our daily lives.

Another tool that we implemented in our investigation at the candle show was the SLS Kinect camera and software that can recognize people by distinguishing body parts, joints and movements. If it shows a person shaped object on the screen that you cannot see with the naked eye then there is something there the IR is detecting and the programing is recognized as a human shape based on body parts and joints together. The figure will appear on the tablet screen as a stick figure in real time. This tool has been featured on countless paranormal television shows and is used by many professional research groups in the field. When we used this tool not only did we detect human figures in the basement that could not be seen by the naked eye but also small animal-like stick figures that in my opinion could resemble monkeys. These smaller stick figures would actually appear on investi-

gator arms and shoulders, one was even touching an investigator's head. The basement was such an extremely active
location, it was like, human and animal spirits were all
around us. If you view the episode you can hear the excitement in all the investigator voices when the stick figures
would appear on the tablet screen.

NJPP Investigator The Ghost History Medium
Kim - SLS Figure

After using the SLS Kinect camera, the team wanted to
try and communicate with spirits using a spirit radio. The
spirit radio that we used during this session was the phasam-
abox. Instrumental Trans-Communication (ITC) research is
an area in this field that is truly amazing to me. It allows the
researcher to ask a question to spirit and receive an intelligent
answer back. There is no way to explain how clear sometimes
the responses are and how critical they can be to a researcher.
With the phasmabox running voices began to fill the basement of the candle shop and gave the impression of many
spirits coming through willing to communicate. I like to
think of these radio sessions as putting a microphone in the
middle of a room with a lot of people in it, so many people
crowded around the microphone singing into it, talking and
making noises. This is what at times the phasmabox session

can sound like, it can be hard to distinguish clear responses. But every once in a while, a voice will come through the device that really makes itself known.

Doctor Richard Slee

There is a point in the episode where the phasmabox session is being conducted and I ask a question. My question is "Is Doctor Slee here with us?" and I can clearly make out a voice coming over the radio that says " Slee " quite clearly.

Summary of the Investigation

The Candle Shoppe of the Poconos is a very unique location, the owners have embraced its history and paranormal activity. They are happy to share their stories of the encounters with the spirits that call the shop home. When speaking with the sales woman Marlana, she spoke with such concern for the spirits of the candle shop. At times she has been caught off guard by the activity but has never felt threatened or endangered by the spirits. It is as if the people at the shop have come to an understanding with the spirits and learned how to coexist with each other. The shop does offer a haunted attraction in the basement and this also features animatronics and some ghoulish displays that will give the unsuspecting tour attendee more than a few scares. I feel that it is all in good fun and keeps people coming into the location, once they are passing through the attraction they will see information on the actual work and people that were the pioneers of medical research in swiftwater. In all honesty if it was just a museum for medical vaccine research, how many people would actually visit? The owners of the shop are keeping the memory alive and people paying to walk though the history of Swiftwaters past. When walking through the shop and getting to see the rooms of Fisher home one can't help but feel spirit all around, the upstairs rooms that once was a backdrop to the daily routines of the family. They are now full of unique merchandise and of course many different varieties of candles.

Myself and the New Jersey Paranormal Project did document what we feel to be paranormal activity happening at the location. We feel we captured audio, video and motion from our devices that really could not be explained and in our opinion was paranormal in nature. The mediumship that was conducted for the investigation really matched up to the historical accounts of the area and the people involved at the location. It's always a fantastic experience working with Kim The Ghost History Medium, one of the things that really jumped out of her reading to me is that she picked up that the spirit that was coming though at the location was a southern gentleman. When doing research on the Fisher family, I discovered that William Redwood Fisher was from Mobile, Alabama. When things like that line up, when mediumship and historical fact connect, it's enough to turn any skeptic into a believer. This is a location that should be investigated frequently and researched by investigators in the field of paranormal. It would be interesting to see what more evidence could be collected over time, especially in the field of ITC (Instrumental Trans-Communication) ITC researchers use radio devices to establish connection to spirit conducting EVP sessions and using radios especially designed for spirit communication. I feel that the spirits of the candle shop have more to say and would be interested in returning in the near future with more tools and experts in the field to document the activity. As for now if you ever find yourself in eastern Pennsylvania, make sure you visit the Candle Shoppe of the Poconos. It's a beautiful shop that embraces it's paranormal history and is a true treasure of the Pocono Mountains.

Candle Shoppe of the Poconos

i just called to say i love you

OUR LOVED ONES are always close and at times let us know that they are still involved in our lives, even though not physically. Spirit energy is all encompassing and when we pay attention to the signs that spirit puts in our paths can be very beautiful and meaningful. We can still communicate with the souls that have gone before us, our loved ones are only a thought away. There are ways to honor them by cooking dishes that remind you of them and share stories that you fondly remember. It's not crazy to even have a conversation and let them know what's going on in the family, remember that our thoughts when directed towards the spirit are like a phone call to heaven. You can even ask for signs from spirits and when received could be a beautiful experience. One of the most powerful signs I ever received from spirit was from my grandmother Louise. I remember sitting in the funeral home and looking at her in the casket. The conversations that we would have on afterlife and how spirit contact would work, came flooding into my mind. She was very open to the paranormal and had many experiences in her life. She was also very intuitive and I feel that is where my abilities have come from, there are so many stories from her side of the family pertaining in seances and communication with the dead. So here I am in the funeral home and I thought to myself is it too soon to ask for a sign? Mentally I started a conversation in my head with her and it went something like this. "Grandma, can you give me a sign that you're ok on the other side". I would receive a sign a few hours later and it was as clear as day to me.

Sitting at the restaurant that her memorial was taking place at after the burial, the room was filled with the sounds of a restaurant. People's plates and silverware clanking and some low talking coming from the many tables. Sitting at the table and thinking about the service, the radio began to play a very interesting song. Stevie Wonder's I Just Called To Say I Love You filled the room, it's words echoing a message from the otherside.

I just called to say I love you
I just called to say how much I care, I do
I just called to say I love you
And I mean it from the bottom of my heart.

I took that as her response to my sign request and it was beautiful and it was then that I felt the impact of how spirit connects with the living through signs. Now fast forward to my son's christening celebration at a restaurant, the family all together and what songs start to play over the radio. You guessed it, I just Called To Say I Love You.

To fill your heart like no three words could ever do
I just called to say I love you
I just called to say how much I care, I do
I just called to say I love you
And I mean it from the bottom of my heart

This song has really become a part of my life and something I have kept to myself until the writing of this book. It shows the subtle ways that spirits can communicate with the living and let them know they are still with them. Now one might argue that it's just a coincidence and that is fine but I have heard this song play at moments in my life with significance and have accepted it as a sign. Your departed loved ones and guides may communicate with you through a song title or lyric that reminds you of them at the exact time you are thinking about them. They may also try to provide you with clarity and guidance through a series of songs with a resounding theme or message that answers a question you have about a particular situation. I Just Called To Say I Love You is just that for me, it's a message from my grandmother that she is still around and with the family.

Grandma Louise and Me

spirit art communication

Father and Son Reunion

THE MORNING STARTED out like just a normal day, sitting in my office and going over the day's emails and answering messages. As i'm sitting at my desk, there was a knock on the door and a courier from the mailroom was delivering the day's mail to me. I have seen him on occasion and always share the normal small talk greetings but this morning was very different. When he entered my office, I started to receive mental images of an older gentleman, the information started to flow and I grabbed a pen and started to write down what was coming through. He delivered the mail and walked out of my office. At that moment I did not know how to bring up that I felt that his deceased father might be coming through with a message for him. I told myself that I will see him in a few days when he is delivered again to my office and I will share what I received with him.

When the images come to me, I try my best to ask the

spirit to give me evidential details about them that would help communicate to the intended person that it's their loved one. These specific details will help them understand and let me know that in fact it is intended for them.

Are they a man or woman?
Were they young or old when they passed?
How did they pass?
What did they do in life?
How did they dress?
What was their personality like?
What did they like to do?
What things were in their home?
Where did they live?
Show important dates?
Anything meaningful to the reviver?
Any apologies or thank yous?
Injuries or mobility issues?
Signs they are around?

These are only a few of the questions I ask spirit when the connection is made, it's our duty and obligation to spirit to try everything in our power to communicate the best we can with the intended receiver. Where I feel that spirit art really helps in communicating that their loved ones are still with them, is that they will have in their possession a sketch with the likeness of their loved one at the end of the message. This sketch is solid proof that their loved one is indeed still with them. Their loved ones' essence was captured by an individual that has no knowledge of the spirit they are sketching and character traits being conveyed. The details of the spirit person's life would not be known and when this information and sketch is presented, comforts the reviver not just that his loved one is still with him but shows the continuity of life.

When I revive the images, they play like a movie through my mind's eye and once the image is completed, I'll start to write things about the spirit person's life around the image. I always try to get the most detailed information and write it down around the image. The sketch for the courier was complete and I filled the paper with answers and information I felt would help the reviver know who this spirit person was. The day came when he walked into my office, placed his mail on my desk and I started the conversation. It was small talk at first but then I mentioned to him that I'm a paranormal investigator and an intuitive. I explained how I get images from spirit and he was quite open to the idea. I told him the last time he was delivering mail to my office I feel that I connected to someone that I feel was attached to him. I started to describe this man and presented the information that was conveyed to me, as I looked up at the courier I could tell he was deeply affected by the information that was revealed. This was the moment that I knew that there was a connection to the spirit person and himself. I told him that I truly feel that it was his father. The courier took a moment but then told me that the image that I drew captured the essence of his father exactly. The mustache that I drew matched the one he had grown at the time of his death. The two names I received from spirit George and Clarence matched friends he had around his home. The mobility issue I saw was confirmed when the cuirrer told me that his father broke a hip at the end of his life and had issues getting around. There were so many details that I provided that made his eyes fill up with tears of joy, to know that his father was still around him. There was one thing I was happy to convey to the courier, his father said that "he turned out ok". I got a sense of love and pride for his son. I asked him why his father would say that?

Sketch of Couriers father

The courier explained to me that there was a difficult time in his life when he was involved with the wrong crowd and was getting into trouble. He now has a stable job and has been working in the healthcare field for many years. I would agree with his father, he turned out ok in my book too. The courier told me that his father was from Jamaica and that morning when walking to my office he was listening to the old music that his father would listen to when he was a child. Even before me presenting him with the sketch and information his father was on his mind. That's an awesome display of synchronicity and how spirit works, giving us signs in our daily lives. He thanked me for the message and told me that it meant so much to him especially at this time in his life.

Hello Old Friend

Another encounter I had with spirit that was truly amazing was with a coworker. She entered my office and asked me if I could do a spirit art session for her. Talk about getting put on the spot, right? She has been following me on social media and has read my previous books and was really interested to see if anyone would come through for her in a session. I happily obliged and grabbed my pencil and paper and sat in the power to allow spirit to connect with me. When intuitives sit in the power we raise our vibration and hope that spirit lowers there so a connection can be made. The images I began to receive were of a man in his fifties, with black hair. I began to sketch and the image of this man started to appear on the paper. Then I started to write details around the image, to make a connection to the receiver. The details I received are what follows, heart/cardiovascular - age 49 to 56 - very fun personality - life of the party, loved music and dancing, especially salsa music - was not feeling well and knew he was sick but choose not to tell anyone - You feel him around and talk to him - he passed very unexpectedly.

When I conveyed the details, my coworker told me that he was 54 years old when he passed and it was very unexpected. He passed from cardiac issues and was keeping his condition a secret from all his family and friends. She told me that he did in fact love music and was the life of the party and loved salsa music. Again so much that came though, helped her confirm that it was her friend. The message that really was moving was that he conveyed that he knows that she talks to him and feels him around her. She told me that she needed to know this and asked if he was ok on the other side. I explained to her that he knows that she thinks of him often and still asks for his guidance. Our thoughts and emotions are like a phone call to spirit and then know what we're feeling and when we're thinking of them. When we reminisce of the times we spent together and moments that we shared with them in life, we draw their energy close to us. In the end it's the love that we have for one another that survives the physical death and keeps us all connected soulfully. Our friends and loved ones are only a thought away.

Coworkers Friend

Spirit art is created by the intuitive without looking at photographs, descriptions, or prior knowledge of departed loved ones or individuals having the session. The medium must obtain the images and more importantly the essence of the spirit from the otherside. This form of mediumship has been deemed by the finest mediums in the world to be the greatest form of evidential mediumship and provides those receiving the reading with hard, tangible evidence of spirits' presence. There are many ways spirits work through people that have this ability, some psychic artists let spirit control their hands as they draw. Others go into a deep trance and let spirit completely take over, often with their eyes completely closed. Some see images in their mind's eye and they simply draw what they are seeing, without allowing their consciousness to influence or interpet what they think they should draw. I have found that over the years many psychic artists have little or almost no formal training and in some cases have no artistic ability at all. Yet once they link with spirit they are guided to draw works they would have never been able to draw on their own. Always remember that the message comes from spirit, through spirit, to spirit. I am only the vessel for the communication to go through and help deliver the messages to the desired individual.

I have also used spirit art in many of the investigations that I attend and feel that it helps tell the story of the locations. Walking into residential homes, business and even historical locations these sketches help put a face to the spirit or spirits that are at the location. It's such a rewarding and beautiful experience when the sketches match people from the locations past and a connection is made. One of my favorite spiritual teachers John Holland say's "before you reach for your outer technology, reach for your inner technology". It's all about working with and developing your soul's ability to connect with the frequency of spirit. This is what makes some mediums and intuitives so good at what they do. They have perfected their ability to connect quickly with this frequency of spirit. We need to raise our vibration, clear our minds and let go of our personal stuff. It can be hard at first to get quiet and let go of our daily mind chatter but you can work on and develop successful meditations, chanting or even prayers that will help you and your soul connect with spirit.

The spirit world vibrates at such a high frequency that we need to raise our vibration and spirit lowers the to communicate, this is also referred to the blending process. When I connect with spirit, I start by clearing my mind and picturing a white light expanding from the center of my chest. The light continues to grow until it reaches the heavens and infinite space. I then ask for spirit to come close and let me be their vessel to communicate messages of love and light. The entire process of sitting in the power can take as little as a few minutes to link with spirit and open up communication by thinking up and raising your vibration. I have seen and listened to many great sitting in the power recordings that are under ten minutes long and are really effective. Once I link with spirit the images start to enter my mind's eye and symbols are also communicated. These symbols are what I use to get the message across to the individual receiving the message. Some mediums call this using your mediumship toolbox, spirit will use these symbols to get their message across. With every message and sketch I deliver, I'm always in awe at how powerful and beautiful the message from spirit truly is.

Historical Location - Mr. Foster

the shanley hotel

I ALWAYS FIND it so fascinating how book projects come about, this chapter in particular. I remember the first time I heard about the Shanley Hotel was when my good friend, who's a medium and spirit artist , mentioned it to me. We were having a conversation about places my group, the New Jersey Paranormal Project, should investigate and she remembered hearing about the Shanley and it's paranormal activity. I wrote the name down in my notebook and continued to work on projects, a few months went by and I was writing my book Case Files of the Paranormal and needed my notebook. When I opened the book up, the page where I wrote notes on Shanley Hotel was looking me right in the face. I believe in synchronicity and that sometimes the universe and spirit can help intervene in our daily lives and help steer us on our journey. In this chapter I want to share with you the reader what goes into an investigation and our experience at this historic hotel.

Once Case Files of the Paranormal was with my editor, I

began to research Shanley and the area of the Hudson Valley it's located in. I also visited the hamlet of Pine Bush, New York and learned about it's paranormal history. The town of Pine Bush is only a short ride away from Napanoch. Pine Bush even has the UFO and Paranormal Museum and embraces the activity that has been reported in this area for decades. The locals from this area of Ulster County, New York shared with me many strange encounters that they had while going about their daily lives in the area. These stories involve UFO's, Extraterrestrials, Sasquatch and of course Spirits. This area of the Hudson Valley is full of folklore and stories that have been handed down for generations.

When I begin to work on my research for a location like the Shanley I want to know as much as I can about the history and land. In some cases even the folklore of a general area can help with getting to know the location's history and paranormal claims. Sometimes when dealing with legends, they get adapted into the paranormal activity reports of an area and can lead to false leads. We as investigators need to sift through the legends and through our research document the evidence that we discover. Intelligent researchers are those who do their homework and come in with a great deal of knowledge on the locations backstory and history. The history of the Shanley Hotel was immense and also played a part in many people's lives. The hotel had seen the best of times and the worst of times, had seen people fall in love and some taken by death way before their time. It was a bordello and speakeasy and where it's owner suffered a fatal heart attack. This book started just as a research project but became something more. I want you, the reader, to come with me and my team and explore the Shanley Hotel with us. I want you to read it's history and get to know the lives of the people that called Shanley their home and the people that visited this historical location. Just as a researcher does, I want you to get to know the area's rich paranormal history and most of all experience the hotel through these pages. When I finished my research on the hotel I felt closer to all these individuals that called the Shanley home. It's time for you to check into the Shanley Hotel and meet it's spirits. We come with the utmost respect and intentions on telling your story and communicating with you. We come here out of love and peace and only wish to have a conversation with you.

CENTRAL SQUARE, NAPANOCH, N.Y.

hudson valley's past

I FIRST BECAME familiar with the area around 2006 when a friend and I discovered Minnewaska State Park Preserve and hiked a very long loop trail on the Shawangunk Ridge. The mountains and cliffs offer amazing views of the Catskill mountains and the surrounding terrain. One can't help but feel a connection to the earth when you're taking in these stunning views and admiring the rock formations. The rocks of the Shawangunks are made up of sedimentary conglomerate and sandstone, with a small amount of shale. They also contain quartz and this area eroded from the Appalachian mountains over several million years ago. When researching areas of paranormal activity, I always like to look at land on which the events are taking place. By starting out an investigation from the ground up, you are able to determine if perhaps earth elements could be at play in adding to the paranormal activity. Theories that paranormal activity manifests at a particular location and uses the elements at the location to boost and aid the activity.

The geology and hydrology of a location can influence and offer the activity an easier way of manifesting. These hypotheses include tectonic strain, stone tape, running water, and magnetic anomaly theories. This area is made up of a perfect storm to act as a booster for this activity to manifest. Quartz can transform energy from one form to another, it can convert mechanical forces into electrical signals. It also has the capacity to absorb, store. Release and regulate energy. The spiritual significance of quartz is it increases your spirituality, awareness, wisdom and inspiration. Sandstone indicates a relatively high energy environment as well, this was very interesting to learn of this area. A study by Lindsey Danielson of Resource Analysis, Saint Mary's University writes that haunted locations were more common within suitable proximity to faults, going up 53% and containing quartz 26%, this could explain the area's paranormal activity.

Driving along Shawangunk Ridge State Park, heading east for about twenty minutes you will enter the hamlet of Pine Bush, New York. This town is no stranger to paranormal events and even boosts its own museum dedicated to the subject matter. Over the years this area of the hudson valley has seen unprecedented UFO activity and encounters with extraterrestrials. Some reports from witnesses have seen glowing orbs emerge from the ground and shoot up into the night sky. One witness even reported to feel a rumbling from deep down in the earth, it vibrated his entire being. Books have been written about the phommonoma, Night Siege, The Hudson Valley UFO Sightings by Joseph Allen Hynek, Philip J. Imbrogno, Bob Pratt and explores the cases. Another researcher that has many books on the paranormal activity in the area is Linda Zimmermann, her years of research and dedication to the phommona is echoed in all her books. Talking to locals of the area they will explain to you that this area of the Hudson Valley has portals and vortexes that offer entryways in and out of this realm into the next, some witness even reported hearing voices and seeing beings emerge out of thin air. As I delved into these reports and talked to people that experienced this phonnoma it's quite incredible to fathom. Could this be a mass hallucination caused by high Electromagnetic Fields, they have been known to cause paranoia and the feeling of being watched.

I would have to side with the paranormal on this one, I personally feel that there is something more to this activity in this region. There are also theories that high EMF can also work just like the earth elements, quartz and other significant geology components in aiding the activity to manifest, like a booster. Inter-dimensional travel via vortexes in this region has been suggested by researchers. Could the veil between other dimensions be thinner in the Hudson Valley? Legendary ghost hunter and paranormal researcher Hans Holzer believed the veil between this world and the next was thinner in the Hudson Valley. He felt that it was more susceptible to paranormal activity. He had many case files from the area and investigated the area frequently. There is little scientific or mathematical ability to measure or discover these locations but theories abound on how they influence places of paranormal activity.

Theories from researchers that focus on this topic are quite interesting. Could the veil between other dimensions be thinner in this area, I would agree with Holzer and say it definitely could be. Let's explore what energy vortexes could offer to paranormal phenomena, the swirling of earth's energy could act as a booster to those on the other side and in different dimensions. These specific locations on earth contain more earthly energy then other places. One common theory is that energy vortexes can be found where ley lines intersect around the globe. These natural lines make up the earth's electromagnetic field. Energy vortexes are believed to have powerful spiritual properties or be highly conducive to spiritual activities like prayer, meditation, and healing. I feel that spirit is energy and they could certainly use these areas to boost their energy and communication. The hudson valley is full of ghostly and paranormal tales that have been reported for generations. From the tales of Washington Irving to the many paranormal investigators that have written about and shared their experiences and research. No one can deny that the area is full of paranormal history. The area has a mystique to it and has been one of my favorite places to investigate. I have been involved with many cases in the region and everyone has been really incredible.

In researching the area a strange encounter was associated with Henry Hudson the english sea explorer and navigator during the early 17th century goes something like this. On September 3rd of 1609, Henry Hudson sailed the Half Moon into the mouth of the great New York river that later bore his name. The explorer and his crew journeyed north for several days, trading with the native residents and searching for the fabled northwest passage to the Orient. By the time he reached the area that would become present-day Albany, Hudson knew that he had not found the passage for which he sought. Reluctantly, he turned the Half Moon and sailed back down the river. That night, Henry Hudson and his crew anchored the Half Moon in the shadow of the Catskill Mountains. Around midnight, Hudson heard the sound of music floating across the mountains and down to the river. Taking a few members of his crew, he went ashore and followed the sound up and up into the Catskills. The sound of the music grew louder as Hudson and his men marched up to the edge of a precipice. To their astonishment, a group of pygmies with long, bushy beards and eyes like pigs were dancing and singing and capering about in the firelight. Hudson realized that these creatures were the metal-working gnomes of whom the natives had spoken. One of the bushy-bearded chaps spotted the explorer and his men and welcomed them with a cheer. The short men surrounded the crew and drew them into the firelight and the dance. Hudson and his men were delighted with these strange, small creatures, and with the hard liquor that the gnomes had brewed. Long into the night, the men drank and played nine-pins with the gnomes while Henry Hudson sipped at a single glass of spirits and spoke with the chief of the gnomes about many deep and mysterious things.

The beautiful Shawangunk Mountains

Stone Chambers

The Hudson Valley is a place shrouded in mystery and folk-lore, ancient stone chambers have been found in this area of the Hudson Valley. These massive stone structures are found in the hillsides and some spelulate are from ancient times. "That's the mystery and adventure, according to this book, *Celtic Mysteries* by Philip Imbrono, the chambers have perplexed researchers of the paranormal and archaeologists for decades." Could these structures just have been used as root cellars for area farmers or where they used for something entirely different? All the chambers are different but have some things in common. For example, all the chambers are made from large stones, and most of them have seven slab stones for roofs. They are usually built on bedrock. Some are recent with regular, smoothly cut stones; some have been modified recently with brick and mortar. The interesting thing is some chambers have been reported to be ancient, based on carbon 14 dating of charcoal. Some chambers allow viewing of specific horizon events. Such as solstices and equinoxes. Could these structures be built on ley lines in this region or even perhaps portals to other dimensions? Could inhabitants from long ago know the mystical power this area in the Hudson Valley has and acknowledge it by building these structures? Glenn Kreisberg wrote in his book "Spirits in Stone: The Secrets of Megalithic America, "I believe evidence exists to support the theory that an ancient cultural group used the terrain and landscape of the Catskill and Shawangunk Mountains to carry out astronomical observations and preserved the information by manipulating the natural terrain to create alignments between landscape features and man-made monuments," he writes in the book.

welcome to the shanley hotel

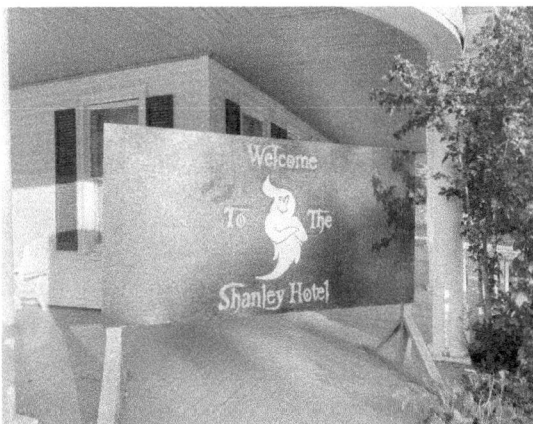

NAPANOCH IS from the munsee dialect of the northern Lenape and is thought to mean land overflowed by water. The Shawangunk mountains that cradle Napanoch have a verbal meaning to the Lenape meaning "it is smoky air" or "there is smoky air. As travelers drive through the streets of this quaint hamlet nestled in the Hudson Valley, they will find a historic bed and breakfast that is a meca for paranormal activity. This location has several famous spirits associated with it and some not known inhabitants. There are claims that the location has portals that allow spirits and beings from other dimensions to enter at any given time. The hotel even warns it's guests that they might have encounters of the spirit kind while staying there. Before we move into the present day, let's examine its history and possible spectors that could be still at the location long after their deaths.

The year was 1845 and Thomas Ritch erected Ritch's Hotel on Main Street. Napanoch was a vacation destationation and a place where people could get away from the hustle and bustle of city life. The railroad was also a benefit to this area bringing travelers from near and far. The Thomas Ritch Hotel boosted the area's best food and furnishingings, weary travelers experienced the area and the hospitality that Ritch provided. When Ritch sold the hotel in 1851 the hotel changed its name to Hungerford's Hotel. As the years passed it still held its reputation as one of the most beautiful, roomy and comfortable hotels to be found in any section of the country. The owner Mr. Hungerford catered to the same clientele that Ritch drew to the hotel, including an elite gentlemans's club that boasted a very distinguished membership and provided ladies for entertainment and enjoyment. This elite group of men enjoyed the benefits of the bordello and the ladies of the night.

The hotel changed hands over the course of the next few years and in 1887, Adolph Wagner became the new landlord and not much was written from this eight year time period. On March 18, 1895 a nearby home caught fire and it quickly spread. The burning embers found their way to the Shanley and the entire structure burned to the ground. Adolph Wagner rebuilt the hotel really quickly after such a total loss and by November of the same year the new hotel emerged from its ashes. James Shanley immigrated to New York City from Ireland, James and his brothers found great success in opening restaurants and hotels across the country. When Shanley discovered the quaint town of Napanoch and the hotel he quickly purchased it on October 1st, 1906. Shanley improved the hotel by adding some of his own personal touches like adding a billiard room, barber shop and bowling alley. James Shanley was truly loved by the community and his name brought prestige to the area. He helped bring revenue into Napanoch and the townspeople loved him for that. He was known for having a kind heart and an outgoing personality. Shanley met Beatrice Rowley and they soon both fell in love, they were married at the Shanley on April 26, 1910 and took off to honeymoon in Washington D.C. Upon returning to Napanoch they were met by a parade welcoming them back and the town was happy to celebrate it's beloved Shanleys. With the future looking so bright for this newly married couple, tragedy lay just over the horizon.

The couple faced hardships and still managed to entertain guests and offer exceptional hospitality. The hotel became known for its card games and domino tournaments and also for hosting elaborate parties into the night. Beatrice Shanley enjoyed hosting tea and social card parties. Mrs. Shanley lived in a small town but did not lack fashion and always displayed stunning jewelry. The hotel was a reflection of her style and offered Victorian beds with sheets of satin and silk. Guests wanted to stay at the Shanley and experience it for themselves, such guests as Thomas Edison, Eleanor Roosevelt have stayed in it's many rooms. The Shanley's were even invited to the Inaugural Ball for President Franklin D. Roosevelt. Eleanor Roosevelt and Beatrice Shanley became quite great friends, First lady Roosvelt always had a room at the Shanley when needed.

Like all newlyweds the dream of starting a family was one the Shanley's wanted to make happen. Beatrice wanted a large family and longed for having children of her own. On January 6, 1912 she gave birth to their first daughter, Kathleen. Kathleen Shanley had complications and only lived a short life, passing away six months after she was born. This was devastating and a gut punch to the Shanleys but they did not give up on their dream of children. Beatrice would give birth to two more children, James Shanley, JR who lived only four and half months and William Shanley who died at a little over nine months. The loss of not only one child but three left the Shanleys heartbroken.

Beatrice welcomed her sister Esther and Husband John Faughman at the Shanley and gave them rooms next to herself and James. Beatrice was very close to her sister and had a close bond. Esther was also very kind hearted and well liked among her acquaintances. Even though Esther enjoyed living at Shanley with her sister, she missed the lure of the big city and her friends she left behind to live in Napanoch. She would sit next to the mahogany telephone booth and wait for calls from her friends back home in New York, City. Then the year 1918 settled on the town of Napanoch, just like the white smoke of the mountains that carddle it, could not protect it from the influenza. Esther fell ill and never recovered and died. The Shanleys had become familiar with death and it's grib that it seemed to have on their family. In the wake of Esther passing away, the Shanleys raised her two young daughters as their own. James Shanley's barber Peter Greger also had a tragedy strike at the location. When his young daughter, only three years old, wandered across the street from the hotel and fell into a well. She struck her head on the rocks as her body fell into the darkness. Her lifeless body was recovered over two hours later, Peter and his family could not stay at the Shanley no more. He gathered his wife and remaining daughter and moved to Brooklyn, New York. He left the darkness and death of Shanley behind him.

The Hotel would see another tragic event unfold in 1915, when Dr. Walter Nelson Thayer, Jr. was baking out of an alleyway that ran between his home and the hotel. Thayer's five year old son jumped onto the car's running board and slipped onto the ground. Not seeing what happened, Thayer continued baking the car out of the ally and ran the boy over with the car. The boy suffered severe head injuries but did not die from the incident. Unfortunate events seemed to happen at the Shanley, one could think that maybe the land was cursed. When the 18th Amendment prohibiting the transportation and the sale of alcohol in the United States happened, James Shanley found ways to keep his clientele happy. The apartment that Shanley rented to his barber Peter Greger and family, now became a bordello and the ladies of the night were back in business at the Shanley. It was like history repeated itself and the morals of the Ritch Hotel creeped back into the building. The dark decision of Shanley letting these deeds go on in his hotel, made many wonder if his wife Beatrice had any objection to it. We don't know if she did but one could imagine that it had to bother her. The once beautiful hotel began to get a new reputation for bootlegging and prostution. The relationship between known bootlegger John Powers and James Shanley is recorded at this time and the two kept illegal sweet nectar hidden beneath the bar through a trapdoor.

One could argue that all the heartbreak and unluck caused James to accept this new reality of the hotel, gone are the days of stately guests and visits from the roosevelts. The hotel perhaps changed the man, the darkness took over his soul. On February 26th 1932 a raid occurred at the hotel, it led to the confiscation of the alcohol and the arrest of John Powers and James Shanley. They both were arraigned in court and both did not have to serve any time. The friendship to Roosvelt and the connection the Shanly had with the town might have come into play at this time. They were let off with a slap on the rest by law enforcement. In 1937 James Shanley suffered a massive heart attack and died, leaving his wife, family and community heartbroken. Beatrice received letters and flowers, wishing her the townspeople condolences for the loss of James. Eleanor Roosevelt sent a letter to Beatrice expressing her sorrow of not learning of his death till after the funeral. The events of Shanleys later life might have also led to the absence of Roosevelt at the funeral, one could speculate. In 1944 it was time for Beatrice Shanley to let go of the hotel and all of the memories that it held good and unfortunately bad. She sold the hotel to Allen H Hazen and he took over the operations. At this the silent room gained its moniker, if Allen had taken part into too many spirits, the beverage kind he would sleep it off in this room. The staff would have to tiptoe around him as he slept off the night's spirits. Hazen ran the hotel until his death in 1971 and in the passing years the hotel changed ownership and names. The most memorable name was the James Shanley Tap Room. In 1991 it closed its doors and was abandoned for over ten years, leaving the spirits within its walls and grounds to themselves. Then in 2005 Salvatore Nicosia bought the abandoned property, just like James Shanley, Nicosia had a vision and a heart of gold. He took it upon himself to restore the building to its former glory. When the property was purchased Nicosia had no idea of the paranormal activity that was happening at this location. It was only a matter of time before the spirits of the Shanley would make themselves known to Salvatore Nicosia.

The hotel always found a way ro resurrect itself and come back, the devastating fire of 1895 that burned the hotel down to the ground. The tragedies that befell its inhabitants and the darkness that also resided in the shadows. The hotel was brought back to life at the hands of Nicosia and he restored it to its former glory. He poured his heart and soul into the project and opened its doors to guests wanting to spend a night at the historic Shanley Hotel. Salvatore Nicosia passed away in July of 2016 and yet again the hotel fell on uncertain times. In 2017 the hotel was condemned and sat empty, the management failed it's guests and spirits. Lucky in 2018 the location was purchased and reopened under new management and yet again has found a way to welcome guests back to the Shanley. Today the Shanley Hotel embraces its historical and paranormal past and offers programs for paranormal investigators. Guests can stay the night if they dare and try to communicate with the spirits at the Shanley. The spirits are just as excited to have it's doors open and rooms inhabited by the living again.

Spirits of The Shanley

Reports of the spirit activity at the Shanley Hotel have been reported numerous times over the years as guests checked in and out with experiences to report. A location that had so much tragedy take place behind it's walls and grounds, would have to hold some form of residual energy of the lives lived and lost there. The shanley not only has residual energy but also has its fair share of intelligent spirits looking to communicate. Perhaps they don't want to leave the beloved property or still feel that they have obligations to the hotel. Hotel guests over the years have captured both phonnonma. I have watched countless videos and audio recordings from paranormal groups and have visited the website for the shanley and have seen compelling evidence of spirit activity. It's a very active location and the spirits want to communicate.

Types of Activity

Residual: A residual haunting can happen when events are recorded energetically at the location, this would be like watching a movie over and over again. This scene that's being repeated over and over again, will not have intellagne. It would be like watching the spirit walk down a staircase and not notice you and go about the same activity and motion repetitively. These locations can absorb emotions during life and death and record them almost into the fabric of time. If the right conditions exist, play them back, like a needle playing an old vinyl record. Locations can act like giant storage batteries and hold these recorded impressions, sounds and images from the past. There are many theories on how this phonnona can occur and I find all of the research to be fascinating. Just the idea that environmental elements are capable of storing traces of our human experiences, thoughts and emotions is mind blowing. This is why when sensitive individuals walk into locations you can feel emotions of what transpired, even if it was a recent argument. I have walked into locations and immediately have picked up on a dark heaviness or light happiness at places I have investigated. Could we be tapping into this residual energy? I personally believe we all have this ability to feel this energy and interpret it. The Stone Tape Theory and Psychometry is very real and spirit energy can be felt and tell its story through objects and locations when visited and touched. I feel that human energy can imbed itself, through a person's lifetime at locations. As a result the lingering energy stored at locations in the future might be played back. People in the future could experience seeing a type of "recording" of these events.

Residual cases that would fit this description would be hearing a woman carrying in a room, nothing changes over time. It's just the same encounter being reported with no interaction. This could also be the case of seeing a spirit walk through a doorway and stand looking out a window, the spirit does not notice you and repeats the same action, over and over again.

Intelligent: As the name implies, this type of haunting has intelligence, or consciousness associated with it. The deceased individual acknowledges your presence and it's not repeating the same actions, like residual spirit energy. It can respond to questions, react to trigger objects, and interact in many ways with the investigators. You could also feel touched and grabbed from intelligent spirits, they acknowledge your human presence. I have been a part of some amazing spirit radio sessions and have obtained evidence from spirit that has answered historical questions I asked. I feel Shanley has so much of the two listed types of spirit communication. These spirits have personality and an understanding and can interact with situations in the surrounding environment. At times even the movement of objects and knocking can occur as a way of them trying to communicate.

Meet the Spirits

Beatrice Shanley
The spirit of Beatrice Shanley has been said to walk the halls of the hotel perhaps looking for her children. She is described wearing period clothing and the smell of fragrant perfume is associated with her.

The Little Girl
The spirit of a young girl has been seen and heard by visitors and has been heard speaking to them from the shadows in the hallways of the Shanley.

The Boy in the Attic
Over the years the spirit of a young boy has been said to

inhabit the attic, the name associated with him is Jonathan. He is said to play in the attic and might have been the victim of a car accident close by. Could his spirit have been drawn to the hotel to reside in the afterlife?

John Powers

Some say that bootlegger John Powers never left Shanley and still lingers in it's dark corners, maybe still trying to indulge in booze and the ladies of the night.

Rosie

This precious little girl's spirit is said to go about the hotel playing and giggling.

Esther Faughman

Beatrice Shanley's sister who died of influenza in 1918 is said to be seen and felt on the second floor of the hotel.

Andrew Shanley

James Shanley's brother Andrew passed away in the hotel in 1919 and some claim have communicated with his spirit.

Speakeasy and Bordello

There are many spirits associated with this time period in the hotel's history and in spirit at the hotel. The spirit activity ranges from prostitutes, mobsters and bootleggers that called the Shanley home.

Anna

Anna worked at the bordello and entertained the gentleman, her room is said to be inhabited by her spirit.

Ghost Cat

Yes, you read that right. The Shanley has a ghost cat that has been caught on camera, walking in it's hallways and rooms.

Besides the listed spirits there are many more that have been reported by paranormal researchers that have encountered the activity. The Shanley has been a mecca for paranormal enthusiasts and guests who want to experience spirit activity. It has been featured on national television shows and is well known in the paranormal community. This is a place that welcomes those with an open mind and let's them step back in time and let's them check into the Shanley Hotel for a night they probably will never forget. As the smoky air from the Shawangunk mountains settles on the hamlet of Napanoch, it's spirits want to communicate, if you want to listen.

As I began researching the area and the history of the historic hotel, I could not help but keep digging into the stories and encounters that guests and investigators have reported over the years. As an author I felt compelled to keep writing it's story and I felt a connection to all these souls that revealed themselves to me through historical information and peoples personal accounts. My paranormal investigation team, the New Jersey Paranormal Project and I would be investigating Shanley in the coming weeks. After my research I feel that I have come to know the Shanleys and looked forward to being able to be their guest and experience the hotel for myself. In the weeks leading up to my visit at the Shanley I began to see scenes play out in my mind's eye, being a clairvoyant I started to do my best and capture them on paper. It's through spirit art, I try to communicate and capture the essence of what I'm seeing in my mind. These scenes play out like a silent movie or at times I'll see symbols and do my best to dephysifer them and put meaning to the symbols I see. One of my heroes and physic mediums John Holland calls it using your mediumship toolbox. It's very true spirit is extremely intelligent in coming through and getting their message across and will use the intuitive the best they can to get their voice heard. This is through imagery and using symbols that the intuitive can interpret and present to the sitter. Everytime I connect to spirit I find this process to be simply amazing.

Through my mind's eye I watched scenes play out and the Shanly at the best of times and the worst of times. I saw happy moments and times of great sorrow that happened to its inhabitants. This was a place where lives were lived and unfortunately for some, came to an end. As I prepared for this trip, I knew this would be an investigation my team and Myself would never forget. It's investigations like this that test all of the researchers involved and really shows your work ethic. Also it's extremely taxing on all the sensitives

lights, camera, spirits

WITH AN ACTIVE LOCATION like the Shanley Hotel it's only a matter of time before it's reputation got out on it's spirits that call this location home. It has been featured on many paranormal shows and many investigators have filmed their experiences and posted them on YouTube. One of the paranormal shows, Ghost Lab featured the Shanley on an episode, entitled Eternal Home that aired in 2010. It's investigators Katie Burr, Barry Klinge and Brad Klinge along with their team documented some interesting evidence during their time at the Shanley. At that time the new owners were renovating the hotel and restoring it, the construction workers began to have experiences and share them with the new owners. One construction worker that was interviewed stated that he has seen dark shadows move all over the building. He also heard the jiggling of keys as if some unseen spirit was unlocking doors. He also heard his name called, only to turn around and see no one there. While investigating the gentlemen's parlor where guests have reported the feeling of being touched and spirits laying in bed with them, Barry Klinge felt as if someone touched his head.

They captured amazing evidence and one EVP that stands out is a deep male voice that was recorded saying "My Home". They believed the voice belonged to past owner James Shanley. Other notable paranormal investigation shows filmed here including Ghost Hunters and experienced Shanley's activity. When you comb through all the YouTube footage that features numerous investigators featuring the evidence they collected during their Shanley investigations, it's simply amazing. The Electronic Voice Phenomena that has been recorded in various locations throughout the home is validation in itself of spirits attached to this location. Now add the physical encounters of being touched and grabbed and seeing apparitions vanish into thin air and you can understand why this building has gained such a reputation with the paranormal community.

Linda Zimmermann paranormal investigator and author of over thirty books on the subject matter, recalled that a skeptical NPR reporter was interviewing her in the basement, freaked out and it's still one of her fondest memories of her ghost hunting career. She also said that some of her most intense experiences occurred at the Shanley.

Ghost Hunters filmed at the Shanley, the hotel was featured on the October 5th 2011 episode entitled "Well Horror". The investigation noted shadow activity on the third floor of the hotel. The team lowered a video camera in the well that Rosie died in and was able to capture the water rippling. They also captured compelling EVP'S and made this a memorable episode of the classic television series.

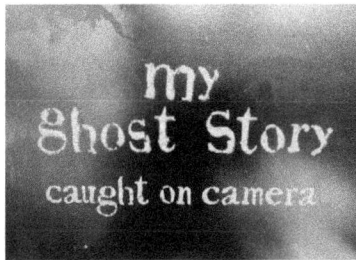

My Ghost Story also featured the Shanley Hotel and had a team investigate it for the television show in 2013. They captured anomalies in photographs and recorded EVPs in the hotel. They also reported feeling physical contact with the unseen spirits of the Shanley. The episode only devoted a segment that focused on Shanley and did not go into great detail of the accounts from over the years. It did however get the location featured again on national television. The allure of a hotel with spirits residing in it's rooms and hallways always finds a way to captivate people with a curiosity for the paranormal. It almost has a Stephen King feel to it, all of it's haunted history and brings to mind his novel The Shining and the way spirits lingered behind it's walls. On Youtube I watected the investigation SCARED that Brian Cano conducted at the Shanley with his team and they caught some very interesting evidence. It was also a great investigation because they combined mediumship with science to validate the activity. As long as the building is standing and guests keep checking in, the spirits that reside at the Shanley will keep making their presence known.

Preparing for the Investigation

When preparing for our investigation, I comed through countless hours of video footage and podcasts of other researchers and teams discussing the activity they experienced. This activity is noted and I bring this along for cross reference for my team members. This location has a wealth of information available to the public and researchers. All these reports help us go into the location with an understanding of activity and names associated with the spirits for our mediums to validate through their walk through of the property. I like to have this information ready in case any of the intuitives come up with names or events that happened. This helps us validate the history with the paranormal. These files are available for the team to access during the investigation.

The way I approach opening up conversation with spirit is not to provoke or antagonize, my team is well aware of this behavior when investing with me. I will not accept anyone trying to push spirit to have a conversation or make physical contact if they do not wish. The fact that some people forget is that ghosts were once people too. How would you like people bursting through your front door, demanding you tell them personal information about you? As these people walk through your home, they get pushy with questions and raise their voices at you? I know you wouldn't respond very well to that experience. This same idea is applied to the way we investigate, when arriving at a location we first start by introducing ourselves and present our intentions for our visit. I feel when dealing with spirit, your intentions are everything. I feel they can feel if you're coming from a good place and possibly let their energy connect to yours. When you start your conversations with spirit, tell them a little about yourself. Then instead of asking about when they died, ask them about when they lived. A location like the Shanley that's so popular with investigators, you can only imagine how many times it's spirits have gotten asked the same old questions. Try a different approach and be more mindful that these spirits lived lives and experienced happiness and sorrow at this location. A more human approach and good intentions will help spirit open up to you and hopefully let the conversation process begin.

When putting a team together for my investigation of the Shanley, I wanted to get a well rounded team in all aspects of paranormal research together. I wanted a team that would all complement each other and work together in telling the story of the locations and it's spairts. In researching the paranormal I have a decent roster of professionals in the field that work great and bring so much to the NJPP Team. I depend on their professionalism and dedication to their area of paranormal expertise. I have surrounded myself with great people to work with and also those with the same intentions that I have in obtaining spirit communication.

October 7th, 2021

My journey to the Shanley Hotel started on an early October afternoon. I left my office and got into my car and made my way to pick up the medium that was joining me at her home. The woman is not only an accomplished medium but a gifted spirit artist, when she communicates with those in spirit she is able to sketch their likeness. It's a truly amazing experience to watch her work and see spirit not only communicate through her but to see their likeness appear on a blank page. As our journey began and we made our way onto the New York thruway, she mentioned to me that she felt a little girl and a barber was connected with this location. I did not want to reveal too much information about Shanley and just told her that the information made sense to me. I continued to drive and we chatted about what we wanted to accomplish on the investigation. The rest of my team, the New Jersey Paranormal Project, was going to be meeting us at the hotel. We also invited ITC professionals Ron Yacovetti and Lourdes Gonzalez to investigate with us, they bring to the investigation another level of expertise. Their area of spirit communication through radio devices and frequencies is amazing and compelling. Another investigator that joined us is Anthony Simonelli of Seekers Club of the Paranormal, his knowledge and years of experience in the field is unparalleled. The team for our investigation for the Shanley all came together and now it was all up to it's spirits to communicate.

As she and I walked up to the front door of the hotel, I noticed the glass sign above the doorway that read "The Spirits Are Inn". The front door opened and we were greeted by our guide for the evening Tracey. She exclaimed welcome to the Shanley and told us to come inside, she was very welcoming and started to talk about the activity that has been recently reported. Her enthusiasm for the subject matter, also gave away that she was a paranormal investigator herself and she shared photos and stories with me of her experiences. The hotel definitely had a feel to it, almost like every room has its own energy. In some rooms light and in others a darker energy permeated the space. My medium began to tell Tracey about Cat's that she was seeing in the location and mentioned one named tiger. You could always see when information being relayed from a medium is accepted just by the mannerisms that the person receiving the message displays. The medium, not being in the hotel for ten minutes already, was being overwhelmed by the spirits of Shanley, she looked at me and said "it's going to be a long night".

As we waited for our group to arrive, she and I stepped briefly out of the hotel and walked across the street to South-wick Square. It's a green space on one side of the hotel that has grass and a tree and a concrete slab that covers a well. This in fact is the well that young Rosie fell down and lost her life. The medium in this area, not even knowing the location of the well and its history, felt a very heavy feeling of tragedy that overcame her. As we stood near the well and looked at it, she immediately said it's a child and did not want to comment much further. She told me later that night that she could see the image of her down there and it was so unsettling. This is a psychic image of the child in the well and is more like a residual imprint left at the location. A life lost so young and tragic still makes investigator's hearts ache with sadness for her and her family. That's an important part of what we do as investigators to always keep in mind that spirits were once people too. We need to approach our communication with them with love and respect. When we do this I feel that our intentions can be felt by spirit and can possibly open the door for communication.

A view from the well, outside the Shanley Hotel

NJPP Investigation The Gentleman's Quarters

The gentleman's quarters at the shanley is located on the ground floor of the building and is conventley located just outside of the door leading up to the bordello rooms. It's a spacious room where the men would gather and take part in card playing and cigar smoking. When the 18th amendment was ratified by the requisite number of states on January 16, 1919 the room even became a Speakeasy. One could only imagine the events that could have transpired behind the hotel's walls at this time. We were informed that this room has an extreme amount of activity and would be a great place to begin our investigation. We set up our equipment and positioned the GS2 laser projection system with it's array of sensors to detect spirit. The Medium immediately started to connect with spirit and Marci also felt that she made a connection with her dowsing rods. The Laser grid began to show movement and varying temperature changes in the projected grid. The medium kept hearing the word Gold mentioned in this space, she sat in the laser grid as she connected with spirit and you could see a significant temperature change all around her. She was glowing red dots on the screen of the lazer, while blue dots fluttered around her.

When doing area research on the possibility of Gold having something to do with the history of the Shanley, Kim discovered this interesting fact. In 1898 four men, Milton, Manny, Fred and George Gosselin were walking in the woods behind the eastern New York Reformatory, then under construction. They came upon a rock that seemed to contain gold, once it was tested it proved their hunch was a good one. It was indeed gold and the thought of striking it rich gave the men gold fever. In 1903 the Napanoch Gold Mining Company was incorporated with the capital stock of $500,000. Unfortunately the gold value did not materialize and the dream of striking it rich disappeared. George

Gosselin did own the Shanley Hotel at this time and is listed in 1900 as the owner of the property. Then in 1906 James Louis Shanley buy's the hotel for $10,000, perhaps Gosselin's misjudgment of his gold venture and the dissolvement of the Gold Mining Company was his reason for selling the hotel.

Napanoch Gold Mining Company

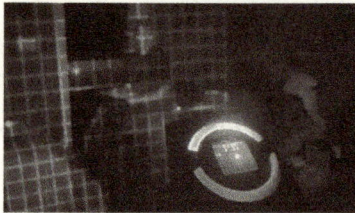

GS2 laser projection system with medium in center.

From visual disturbances to environmental changes the laser grid documented so much activity in the gentleman's quarters, just having the medium get the word Gold is so interesting to me for its connection to a moment in time. It's experiences like this that help peel back the layers and validate our connection to spirit.

The Basement

As we descended into the basement of the Shanley, you could see the old fondation and dirt floor come into view. That old smell of musty wood and dirt hit you immediately, as we tried to look around to get a sense of our surroundings. On the left was a long tight room that had a red chair in the center of it. This room was where Tracey said they had seen a hooded figure standing. Tracey informed us, this would be a great place to experiment with the Estes Method and see if we could engage in conversation with spirit. The Estes Method is to further isolate and concentrate on the random radio feed. One must have the SB7 Spirit Box Or spirit radio tapped into soundproof headphones (so they cannot hear the questions being asked) and be blindfolded (so they cannot guess/read lips at what is being asked). Once this has been established, the other investigators in the room (not the person listening) ask questions and see if the radio snippet of the human receiver matches. The human receiver says out loud any words or phrases they can make out. This technique has been very interesting for the results that it gets at many haunted locations. It also has been featured on the television show Kindred Spirits and has become a very popular technique for paranormal investigators. Greg Newkirk of Week and Weird and Hellier shares his own thoughts on the method, "Having seen and utilized the Estes Method myself, the results are nothing short of stunning, and that's coming from someone who loathes all forms of spirit boxes, radio sweeps, and "random" speech generators used by paranormal investigators. The brilliant part about the Estes Method is that it effectively removes the "group bias" of spirit boxes, a side effect which taints their usage."

I volunteered myself to sit in the long dark room off the basement and try my hand at the estes method. The room is so narrow that I could touch both sides of it with my hands, I could really notice if anything went by me. I positioned myself in the chair and was handed the SB7 Spirit Box and soundproof headphones, the room went dark and blackness was all around us. Through the radio static words emerged that were completely random and I spoke them out loud to my team members. At one point during the experiment I felt an overwhelming feeling of grief and sadness come over me, at this time Hayden Keck was holding a thermal camera and noticed a light source that was moving around me. The light source appeared around my head and then quickly vanished. It was very interesting that that feeling and the light source happened about the same time as we were conducting the experiment.

The basement is such an interesting place and even has an old wooden casket that was converted into a cart by a previous owner. It's a place where you can totally feel energy peering out from it's shadows and observing you. The team also used lights that indicated movement and had them triggered by an unseen presence. Our medium Kim was able to pick up on a great sadness in the basement and mentioned babies, african american man and the name Patrick. The location also is alleged to have been a stop on the underground railroad and could have been a temporary stop for slaves seeking freedom in the north. Kim also mentioned feeling a mysterious energy swirling around a pile of stones on the floor of the basement and felt immediately dawn to sit by them. The entire time the team was in the basement, it seemed to come alive with activity. I would have to say the experiment of the estes method was a great success and I truly feel that I had a personal experience with spirit in that dark corner of the Shanley Basement. There also is the possibility that the basement could have been the resting place for victims of the mob involvement at the Shanley. This could also be a place where secrets of the bordello could lay buried under rock and dirt. Hard evidence that was obtained by investigators suggest that people could have been murdered in this space.

The basement of the Shanley Hotel and the earth that it sits on, is shrouded in mystery. The events that took place in the space have left a residual imprint and also intelligent spirit activity. You can feel the presence as soon as you descend the stairs and step onto the dirt floor of the basement. It's a very heavy feeling I would say the basement has, there is a feeling of great loss and sadness. I personally will never forget the estes experiment that I participated in and what I felt while doing it. I truly feel that I connected with spirit that night in the basement and spirit let me feel the loss and grief that they felt. As investigations happen and other groups and investigators descend the stairs into the Shanley basement, proceed with respect and love for the spirits that share this space with you. It's important to document your interaction and response to the answers that come from the other side of the veil.

Basement stairs at the Shanley Hotel

Rem Pod Experiment in the basement of the
Shanley Hotel

I feel that the location's activity came in waves and felt different throughout the hotel. As we entered each different area, you would feel a multitude of feelings that went from light to dark. When in it's hallways and silence occurred, you could at times almost hear murmured voices coming from unseen beings. This happened a few times to myself and other team members as we covered the different floors of the hotel. The sound of human voices, as if in conversation with themselves. Some team members even reported hearing phantom footsteps that would be walking towards them and just dissipate. This was very unsettling to seasoned investigators and confirmed how haunted this location is. From the gentleman's quarters to the basement this was an investigation we won't soon forget.

The third floor of the hotel was another location we wanted to investigate and our group chose a room across from another room that was filled with childrens toys. The room was dark and offered a few chairs where some of us could sit during the investigation. I was sitting next to our medium. We all felt that we were communicating with the presence of a man in this room. Some of the group felt that he was somewhat standoffish and possibly irritated, our medium leaned into me and asked if I would accompany her downstairs and get a drink. I did not hear what the medium asked and leaned into her and asked her to repeat the question. As I leaned into the medium, her chair unexpectedly was tipped and she fell out of the chair. I felt the chair move and knew that something with enough force came up from behind the chair and tipped it over. There was no one but our group in the room and there was a wall behind us. It was so chilling to know that spirit actually used force to move the chair. Now we do not feel that the spirit was trying to harm us but in fact possibly got annoyed that she and I were going to leave the room after the spirit started to communicate. You could imagine that spirit must have been like "go get that drink of water now". That's the personality that I feel that this man probably was in life.

We also don't know if spirit gets tired of communicating with various groups that come into these spaces and try to make contact with the otherside. You could only imagine getting asked the same questions over and over again and how you would respond to it. This is why I really enjoy working with Ron Yacovetti and Lourdes Gonzalez, they are experts in spirit radio communication. The two methods that they use to establish contact with spirit, really brings so much more evidence into an investigation. The use of Ghost Boxes or spirit radios that sweep or phonetic devices with only allophones (smallest fragments of human speech), made exclusively by Hultay Paranormal (NJ) and a European method known as DRV: Direct Radio Voice. DRV Direct Radio Voice Session with a VST Software and AI. There is nothing being used from the radio perspective, besides a Longwave Frequency that is barren of radio emissions. Long story short, vocals are not present in the white noise so they should not be in what we are hearing...but they are. And they're responsive.

When you hear voices come through these devices it's simply amazing, when they answer questions intelligently or comment on things happening at the location, that only could be seen by people who are present, totally mind blowing. While at Shanley I gave Ron Yacovetti a copy of my latest book Spirit Voices that he contributed an interview to. I had no idea that spirit would bring this up that night at a later time through a spirit radio session. Through the different techniques that Ron and Lourdes used we are absolutely positive that spirit used the devices to communicate and comment on our presence at the hotel. I feel that spirits must be very curious about the communication process of using their frequency to connect with the radio devices that were implemented. As voices come through the AM-FM band or appear through DRV whitenoise, I wonder if they want to communicate with us, just as much as we want to communicate with them? Are they on the other side of the veil, attempting to make contact with us? From responses I have heard through my research and documented accounts of this area of research, I strongly feel spirit is. The following is a list of what was documented during the spirit radio session that we conducted at the hotel.

- Richard - We Want You Back
- Get Right - To Sleep
- Can't Keep My Eyes Opened
- Allergies
- They're Open
- The Books
- You Forgot to Autograph Them
- Didn't You
- Well Goodnight
- 3 AM

DRV Direct Radio Voice Session

I found the responses to be relevant and also pertained to conversations and events that happened during our time in the hotel. I know while investigating my allergies did act up and I mentioned it to the team. I know that I handed two books to Ron and Lourdes that were not signed, they also did not autograph the books. The investigation ended shortly after three o'clock in the morning and again is relevant for the good night response from spirit at that time. Overall I was really blown away from the documented resources and so grateful that Ron and Lourdes joined us at the hotel.

Time with Maddy

One of the last rooms in the hotel that I investigated was Maddie's room. It's in the bordello section of the hotel. If these walls could talk I'm sure that they would have stories to tell. My team called me upstairs into the bordello area, when my name came through the Phasmabox spirit radio. A voice was heard by the team saying "Get Rich". As I walked up the tight staircase into the bordello area my team was sitting in a small waiting area outside of the dark rooms. The names Anna's Room, Maddie's Room and Rosie's Room were above each doorway. This is where these women entertained the gentleman that visited the hotel and were subjected to who knows what kind of treatment. Being intuitive you could feel the despair in this area of the hotel, this is where they worked day in and day out. They probably wished for a man to come visit the hotel and take them away from this place and far beyond the town of Napanoch. As I approached the door ways, my team pointed to Maddie's room. I walked into the dark room and sat down on the bed. I took money out of my pocket and placed it on the bed.

I wanted to create a situation that happened in that space that spirit would be familiar with. In recreating events that took place at locations they can act as a trigger object in getting spirit to respond. As I sat on the bed and placed the money down next to me, I mentioned that I was visiting the area and I wanted company. The room was completely quiet, no floorboard squeaking, just still. Then as I sat there, looking into the darkness around me I felt something start happening. I began to feel pressure on the bed behind me. Something was starting to sit on the bed with me, I could feel the mattress going down and alerted my team immediately. As fast as the encounter occurred it went away and the room was just still and the pressure was gone from the bed. If it was Maddie, she just joined me for a brief time and made her presence known.

Mirror Scrying

Just off the first floor before you enter the gentleman's quarters, there is a small room on the left that only contains a chair, small table and an antique mirror. The table has small votive candles that light the room just enough for scrying. I entered the room with another investigator and they stood at the door, I sat down at the chair and began to look at my image in the mirror. I softened my gaze and within a minute or two began to notice small differences start to appear in the image that was looking back at me. I noticed that my face seemed to drop and old age lines formed by my mouth. Even the investigator at the door said to me "Rich that is not you at all". It was really jarring to experience but so interesting to me. Being a student of the paranormal and the occult I embrace having experiences like these and learning from them. I feel that intentions and respect of the subject matter is also part of your protection when having these experiences. If there are portals at the Shanley, this mirror offers us the opportunity to glimpse beyond the veil. Mirrors have always had a mystique to them in the paranormal, let's talk about one of the oldest forms of Divination rituals

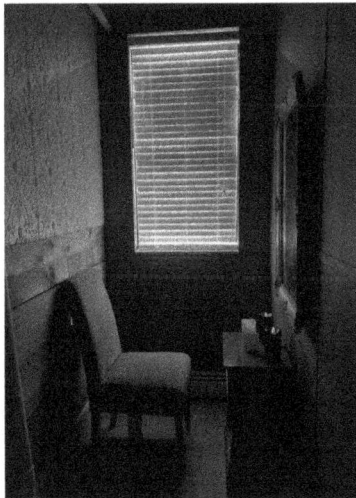

Mirrors have been associated with spirituality for hundreds of years. From covering the mirrors in a home

when someone has died to the belief that in placing mirrors in relation to one another you can reflect images from the other side. Even stories of duality (the other 'you' emerging from the mirror) For example, in one of the cases, a woman looked into the mirror and saw her own corpse staring back at her. There are other accounts of people claiming to see themselves age and change drastically in appearance. Taking part in the act of scrying is an ancient technique of connecting with the otherside. It is suggested that you protect yourself and say a prayer and surround yourself with the white light of protection. Then as you gaze at your reflection in the mirror, a candle is the only light illuminating your face. As the flame flickers, you look into your mirror image and let your scrying experience begin. When you have relaxed completely, work to still your mind from mundane thoughts. Make your mind as blank as possible. Focus on the surface of the mirror and the reflection you see from the candlelight. Do not strain your eyes to see anything or work too hard. Relax and let it come to you."

Shanley Hotel Scrying Mirror

The ancient Mayans believed there were multiple worlds in addition to the human world. Their belief that portals connected these worlds and allowed active engagement between the Maya and their gods. Without portals and the ability to communicate between the worlds the Maya belief system could not function. Evidence suggests the Maya believed reflective surfaces, mirrors and water surfaces, were portals to spiritual worlds. In Judaism mirrors are covered when the living mourn their dead is a belief from jewish mysticism. They believe that different types of evil spirits and demons come to visit a family mourning the deceased. When the soul leaves this world, a void is left behind, that dark forces could take advantage of. This might allow negativity and evil into the home and prey on the family. So in an attempt to protect the living, mirrors in a home that is going though the morning process are covered. These evil spirits cannot cannot be seen by the naked eye and you could catch a glimpse in the mirror. This mystical belief protects the living and offers protection during a very difficult and vulnerable time. When researching mirrors and the paranormal so many cultures have beliefs in the theories that mirrors are portals and could act as a doorway for spirits to enter a home. It makes one wonder with so much ancient and modern text written about mirrors and their paranormal abilities, there has to be some truth to the knowledge being passed down.

Scrying Image of distorted face

spirit art and the shanley

WHEN I WAS PREPARING for the investigation at the Shanley Hotel, I was devouring history and information on the area it's located in. It's important to me to have a very extensive and complete file on the location. Sitting at my desk in my office, as I finished the research for the day. I would meditate and ask the spirit to come close, with paper and pencil in hand I would sketch the images that I received through my mind's eye. The images played like an old movie, one image was of an older man with a fedora who showed him sitting at a table. He was enjoying liquor and playing cards with men gathered around a table, the smoke of cigarettes and cigars left the room filled with a smoky haze. I got a sense that he was respected and received a "J" name associated with him. I saw him dressed in a suite but some of his dress shirt buttons were undone in a casual way. These images came to me and I did my best with my ability to sketch them down on paper. I hoped that at least I could capture the essence of the person and add it to the file. Being clairvoyant it's important to me to do my best in capturing the essence of what I'm seeing and translating it to paper. When it's presented to the sitter or the staff at a location and it fit's a person's description or photo, that's the reward. Spirit is so amazing at communicating and getting it's message through.

Sketch of Shanley Man

Sketch of Shanley Man

ONE MORE IMAGE that came to me for the location, was of a beautiful woman. I saw her in a room at the hotel looking out a window. I could sense a sadness that emanated from her eyes, almost wishing she could be somewhere else other than the hotel. Her brown hair was worn up and she was very elegant and nicely dressed. I would place her in the 1920's or 1930's at the location.

Shanley Woman

Child sketch from the Shanley Hotel

On this investigation at Shanley I was blessed to work with one of my good friends, who is not just a medium but a spirit artist as well. Her work is exceptional, she's a very gifted spirit artist who can capture the essence of spirit. She brings so much experience into an investigation. I have come to know and work with her overtime and have seen her work in the field and think she's such an incredible asset to have on a paranormal investigation. In this field it's important to surround yourself with good people and she is one of those good people. When we arrived at the Shanley it did not take her long before she had pencil in hand and was sketching spirit. The white sheet of paper she held, slowly started to show the essence of a person. The sketches gave us a glimpse of the spirits that call the hotel home. She is a devout spiritualist and is a pleasure to work with, she is full of knowledge and brings so much knowledge to the table in communicating with spirit. Her spirit art is beyond amazing and the three sketches she did at the Shanley are quite impressive.

The sketch of the man with the tie, we felt matched a photo in the main kitchen area. Our guide for the night Tracey pointed him out in the photo. The medium walked over and held the sketch up to the photo to see if his essence was captured. In a situation like a hotel it's so hard to tell with all the various guests that have stayed at the location over time, I must admit that the sketch did really match up to the photo. The little girl sketch was another amazing connection from spirit to paper, long before we pulled up to the Shanley, she was feeling a child spirit coming through. As this sketch began to happen, I could not help but wonder who this child could be. Tracey told us of a child that was murdered associated with the hotel and this could possibly be the essence of that child. The final sketch was of a man with a mustache, she drew his image in the gentlemans quarters. She felt that he was associated possibly around that time period. She also mentioned that he could also have been involved in the nearby gold venture George Gosselin was involved with.

The spirit art from the medium and Myself was created without looking at photographs, descriptions, or prior knowledge of people from the Shanley Hotel. The medium must obtain the images and more importantly the essence of the spirit from the otherside. This form of mediumship has been deemed by the finest mediums in the world to be the greatest form of evidential mediumship and provides those receiving the reading with hard, tangible evidence of spirits' presence. There are many ways spirits work through people that have this ability, some psychic artists let spirit control their hands as they draw. Others go into a deep trance and let spirit completely take over, often with their eyes completely closed.

Some see images in their mind's eye and they simply draw what they are seeing, without allowing their consciousness to influence or interpet what they think they should draw. I have found that over the years many psychic artists have little or almost no formal training and in some cases have no artistic ability at all. Yet once they link with spirit they are guided to draw works they would have never been able to draw on their own. Always remember that the message comes from spirit, through spirit, to spirit. The words of the great medium and spirit artist Coral Polge really resonate with me. "We are purely telephone lines, nothing more," she said. "As long as there is somebody's picture waiting to be drawn, I will continue to be used as a channel for such communication between this world and the next. This was the path mapped out for me. It is a path I tread with love, and a great sense of privilege that I was chosen to do so." It is truly a remarkable experience when this connection occurs and we convey the message and image of spirit.

Mediums Spirit Art Sketches from the Shanley

Man with Mustache

reflection on the shanley

The Ghost History Medium Kim and Richard Moschella

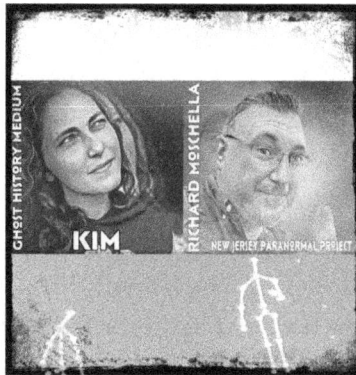

MANY INVESTIGATORS HAVE REPORTED hearing music being played and doors opening and closing on their own. The hotel has a lingering residue of the events that transpired behind its walls. Reports of hearing the banter of a party happening and then hearing the room fall to s ghostly silence. Phantom conversations have been heard by guests and happen quite frequently. Some sensitives have stated that the third floor of the hotel draws them to it and they claim to feel the presence of a young woman who committed sueaside on this floor. It is believed that something that transpired at the hotel, led to her taking her own life. A young young woman in her early twenties, is the description that many senstives have given for this spirit. It is so terribly sad to think that someone so young and with so much life to live would choose this way out. The third floor is also known to have caused people to not feel well and get struck by a sudden feeling of sickness. Reports of people feeling a shortness of breath and being strangled have also been documented. Another account from the third floor is of a medium picking up the presence of a man being bludgeoned to death, his upper body taking blows that would leave him dead.

With over thirty supposed spirits that inhabit the hotel many investigators and sensitives said that when they leave the Shanley they need a few days to decompress from the energy that they encounter at the location. Some have even gone as far to say that they feel as if the hotel had drained their energy and they had to ground themselves when they left. I can say that the hotel has not left my thoughts, since I investigated with my team. Here I am a month later still writing about the Shanley Hotel and reviewing interviews and evidence. I only had the opportunity to investigate the location for one night, in that one night some really profound events took place. These events and the recordings from our spirit radio sessions will forever replay in my mind, when I think of Shanley. This was one of the most memorable experiences of my paranormal career and I hope to return in the future and document more evidence from this incredible location. In a way all that enter this hotel leave a little something of themselves behind when they leave. That energy imprint of their spirit and their time in space. Just maybe when those who investigated and visited the Shanley departed from this world might visit the location in spirit. That number of over thirty spirits might continue to grow. One thing I know for sure is that Spirits are always inn at the Shanley Hotel.

What follows is the post interview between The Ghost History Medium Kim and Myself on reflecting back on the investigation we did at the Shanley Hotel. We hope this offers insight to what we experienced and felt while investigating the historical location.

Kim The Ghost History Medium:Shanley Post Interview

What did you feel or expect walking into the Shanley for the first time ?

I didn't really know what to expect and I didn't know anything other than it was a hotel in New York that has paranormal activity. My experiences started as we were driving into the Rondout Valley. I began experiencing dense energy and body sensations. It felt like the energy was heavy and slow and like I was swimming in an ancient lake or something. This sensation persisted all through driving in the valley, but when we got closer to the town, I started experiencing body pain like gunshots or knife stabbings. At the actual hotel, energetically I was greeted by an entourage of people (about 5 of them) who considered themselves "a part of the family". They were not particularly welcoming but allowed us freely inside. Multiple spirit men were outside at the front door like on watch or bouncer types. There was also a man sitting in a chair on the front deck casually smoking a cigar.

Was there an area that you felt most drawn to?

I am always drawn to the outdoors first at a location. Inside the home I was most drawn to the bedrooms on the second floor down the hall towards the second floor porch, but we didn't investigate that area.

Opinion of spirits at the location?

There are a lot of spirits present. Some that belong and some that don't belong there. "Belonging" would mean that they had a connection to the location in life, aka lived there, died there, stayed there long term, visited, or had a strong emotional connection to the place. Some of the spirits seemed to be passers by or freely welcomed in by the living and not really connected to the place historically.

Memorable Events That Happened?

Going up to the rooms above the gentleman's room I immediately saw small children. Later we investigated further and the spirit of Rosie is said to have lived in that area of the home.

Do you believe that the hotel has portals?

I loved how the reading outside the location spoke of how the energy in the valley is stagnant and slow to turn over. And this was due to the valley being boarded on two sides by north to south running mountain ranges rising abruptly up from the valley floor. Also the geology of this location is important as to why so much paranormal activity is found here. The mountain rock composition includes quartz and limestone, both of which are associated with paranormal reports compared to other rock compositions. How it was explained to me is that energy in this valley has a hard time circulating out because the energy cannot flow well in this valley region. This means that old energy stays around longer leaving the area to have a hard time renovating, changing, or updating. It also means that residual energy from the past may be more present and experienced by the living. The old tends to remain. Old homes stay abandoned and are not demolished for the new and businesses may struggle. This has nothing to do with the economy but is a direct effect of the lingering stagnant energy in the area. Also health may be an issue and feelings of headaches or sluggishness. This occurs throughout the Rondout Valley and there are likely many paranormal occurrences within this whole valley region.

Napanoch the town was founded in 1706 by the

Bevier family, who were French Hugenots. There is a historic marker for the Abram Bevier house about 1-2 miles from the Shanley Hotel. Interestingly I was mentioning beaver pelts as a cause for expanding into this area and said the town was founded in 1720. Albany and the Husdon river were known for their early exports of beaver pelts and for the real success of the fur trade in New Amsterdam. Also beaver sounds a lot like Bevier . . . Anyway, route 209 was used by the Native Americans to travel from the Delaware River to the Hudson River along the ridgeline to the Saugerties area (NOT Syracuse). I mentioned that it was a boundary line between tribes, which it may have been, but it was certainly a boundary line of the Settlers and the Native Amerians. During the 1700s it was considered the Western Frontier and many forts were built on this road in defense. "The earliest mention of the road speaks of it as a " Trade Path." In 1682 it was spoken of as "The Path of the Great Valley." It is mentioned 1737 as the "Mine Road" and in 1770 is spoken of as the "Good Esopus Road."" Davy Crockett may have come up as just another reference to animal furs (his coon hat), or the fact that he too was a French Hugenot, or that he too was significantly associated with "The Western Frontier", he opposed Native American removal from land, or maybe it was because Davy Crockett was born in 1786 in Limestone, TN.

Very interesting. I could not find any direct link to Davy Crockett in Napanoch.

Outside I mentioned mastodon bones in the area or

saber tooth tiger teeth and it turns out 2.5 miles from the hotel a set of mastodon fossil teeth and jaws were discovered in a pond. No saber tooth tiger bones or teeth have ever been discovered in New York.

Outside when I was trying to pick up the years when the hotel was built and picked up one

I was tossing between 1840 and 1860 and when I went back to the 1840s, the camera started acting strange, twice. This was the older man communicating confirming the dates being built of 1840s. The hotel was in fact built in 1845! It was really interesting to pick up on two men in particular similar in appearance and age as to who Dawn picked up in her reading. That was very validating. On the third floor, I clear as day heard footsteps walking towards me in the hallway and then the motion sensor light went on on the stairs going down. Also on the third floor in the first room down the hallway on the left, I encountered a male spirit who was angry and staged a murder. He kept feeling like the aggressor and not the one who was murdered to me. He made me feel very angry, agitated, and upset at everything in life. He hated everyone and everything. I felt like he was a dangerous spirit and had the ability to create the sensations of pushing and choking people. I also got the years of the 1960s associated with this man. Also in this room the meters were going off, strange light phenomena on the cameras, and Dawn's chair was physically moved. I believe portals occur in two ways, they can be naturally associated with land features or are created by the living. They can be created by the living through massive events, or through intentions of inviting spirits in and opening the place to communications.

I did feel that there were many spirits present in this location and multiple spirits who I do not feel are directly associated with the location. I can only explain this as spirits wandering and being attracted to this place for one reason or another. The hotel acts as a beacon and can attract spirits. Maybe this beacon ability is just another word for portal?

I personally did not feel a particular spot or area that had portal-like energy. Portal energy to me feels chaotic, spinning, and like a void. I did not specifically feel this here. I was drawn to the rock pile in the basement as something different or hiding something.

Any encounters in your room, when you went to sleep?

Nope slept like a baby. We did have a camera in our room recording for about 2 hours during the night of the investigation and we captured a few bumps, maybe footsteps, and noises within the room that I cannot explain.

Opinions of the gear that was implemented?

I love technology and I am always happy to use it to communicate with spirit. I love when a voice comes through and I am fascinated that they can have different tones and cadences. I wish we had used more standing cameras in rooms that we were not in to see if we could capture any visuals or sounds. I also wished we used the SLS or heat sensors more as well during the investigation.

ITC AND DRV Radio Session - Results - What did you think of the audio evidence collected?

Very advanced and loved that otherwise the sound was quiet unless something was said by spirit. It was difficult to hear at the moment but very clear to hear the voices and response upon replay. Very cool!

Richard Moschella: Post Shanley Interview

What did you feel or expect walking into the Shanley for the first time ?

I was excited to get into the location and see it for myself, in the weeks leading up to our investigation I felt that I had come to know Shanley and it's cast of characters. I knew it would be an experience and probably an investigation we would not forget.

Was there an area that you felt most drawn to?

The entire building has spirit activity, even walking on the grounds outside the hotel you can feel the location's energy. I really felt drawn to the basement and feel that is where I had one of the most interesting experiences during this investigation. Being sensitive to spirit in a place like the Shanley is like moths to a light, you stand out. It can be an overwhelming feeling for all sensitives who come into a location like this. From my arrival to when we departed, spirit was very much present and observing us.

Opinion of spirits at the location?

In my opinion we were never in any harm or felt oppression from the spirits that inhabit the Shanley. It was more like just meeting different people with varying personalities. There were some nice people and others that might not have been too friendly. When an investigator was tipped out of her chair next to me, it was not done to harm her but more as a spirit trying to get a message across. Before the chair tipped, she told the room of investigators that she was going down stairs to get a drink. I could not hear exactly what she said, so I leaned into her to hear what she was saying. As she began to say for a second time that she was going down stairs for a drink the chair she was sitting on tipped downward. We both felt that spirit might have been annoyed that while they were trying to communicate, she was talking about leaving to get a drink. So this spirit did not want to harm her but made a point like "go and get your drink then". We both were blown away by the encounter.

Memorable Events That Happened

The entire time at Shanley was amazing and really impacted me. Not only in the research but getting to know these people that spent time in the hotel over the years. Then being able to walk in their footsteps and explore the location and enter the rooms that these people lived in. The owners of the Shanley have done an amazing job at preserving its history and it's connection to the paranormal.

Advice for investigating locations

In highly publicized locations like this one it's important to me to have my own experience. I want to go into these locations with knowledge of the events that have transpired but I don't want these other investigations to lead me on my time in the location. I encourage you to go where your gut and intuition leads you. This is what will make your investigation and experience unique to you and your team. It's easy to fall prey to watching videos and reading accounts of the most active places and spend too much time in the areas that other investigators reported to be the most active. Trust your instincts and let spirit guide you, activity is not always predictable and is ever changing.

ITC AND DRV Radio Session - Results - What did you think of the audio evidence collected?

When you are able to ask questions to spirit and get intelligent answers back through radio communication, that to me is some of the most powerful evidence you can collect at a location. On this investigation at the Shanley Hotel,

Ron Yacovetti and Lourdes Gonzalez joined us. They had an assortment of their radio equipment and really concentrated in collecting voice evidence though their devices. When I interviewed Ron for my book Spirit Voices he gave this advice for implementing radio devices for spirit communication sessions. Ron went on to say, the best advice is to learn. Read about it. Watch shows or videos. All content teaches, even if what not to do is an unintentional lesson. Be respectful as you would be, or should be, when engaging anyone you speak to, living or not. Secure your environment as best you can, so you know when you review and think you caught something that it's not a false positive. Mark and tag vocally any possible thing that can be misinterpreted on a recording as a spirit voice. Use devices that resonate with you. DRV proponent Dr. Anabela Cardoso once asked the spirits why, of the four radios she ran during a DRV sitting, they came through one specifically, most of all. The voice response to that question was, "because it is your favorite." Point being, intent and its energy is likely a main ingredient in this whole communication with the so-called dead thing.

The sessions that Ron and Lourdes conduct are always so fruitful in evidence collected and I feel that their approach to spirit is key to their success. I have great respect for all ITC practitioners and feel that they help complete the puzzle when documenting a location's paranormal history.

Spirit Responds to people differently

I have seen this happen many times investigating locations with different individuals. Some of the investigators would be magnetic to activity while others would hardly experience anything. I believe that spirits can be drawn to male and females, they can also be drawn to individuals that have an occupation they had in life, spirit can also sense the intention of the individuals their space and make the call to communicate or not, also I strongly believe that some people are more intuitively open to paranormal activity than others. I have investigated alongside some investigators that through the time we spent together, I have picked up strong intuitive abilities from. This can also be why some people get affected by spirit in different ways.

Soul Communication

We are incarnate beings , while spirits are discarnet beings. This being said is that our physical bodies contain our souls and who we are. Our soul energy comes up from our chest area and expands out beyond our head. Medium John Holland describes our souls as an upside down iceberg, going from our physical bodies upward. When communicating with the spirit world he says to "Think up" our souls that are expanding outward can connect with those souls in the spirit world and blend in frequency. We are putting our thoughts and intentions into our soul and trying to link our soul with spirit. When individuals do this the connection can be made and communication can happen. In my belief this is why spirit communicates with people differently, it all depends on how open and ready to connect you are. This is why mediums and intuitives can walk into a location and almost immediately start firing on all cylinders. They know how to inline their soul frequency with spirits and communicate across the veil.

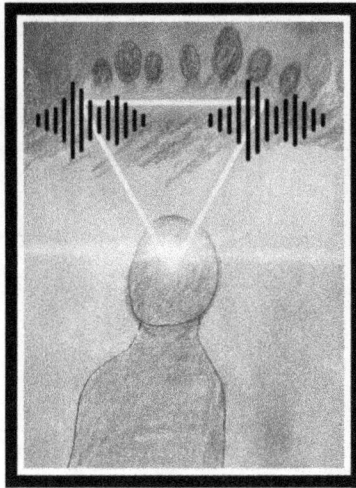

Soul Communication with Spirit

hotel portal and interdimensional travel

IN HARRISVILLE, Rhode Island there is a home that is nestled on a hill in the countryside, the farm on round top road is believed to have extreme paranormal activity and portals.The conjuring film series and the work of Ed and Lorraine Warren popularized it and it's one of the most known paranormal locations in the country and the probably the world.There is so much written about the conjuring home but one book series from Andrea Perron is essential to understanding the activity and experiences. House of Darkness, House of Light is a three volume set that details the encounters the Perron family witnessed, while living in the home. One of the descriptions that Andrea gave of the home, really made me think of the portals at the Shanley Hotel. Andrea described the home as "It's a portal cleverly disguised as a farmhouse. It's multiple dimensions, interacting simultaneously." If the farm on round top hill is cleverly disguised as a farmhouse, could the Shanley be disguised as a hotel and really are doorways to other dimensions.

This theory of the hotel having open doorways for spirits and interdimensional beings to slip in and out of our realm could be very possible. This also could explain why so many different spirits are said to be at the Shanley. Some mediums have stated there are more spirits at the Shanley than people at times. If these portals are allowing beings from other realms passage into the hotel, you can only imagine why it's such an active location. This would also bring more activity into the space and not only from the people who lived or visited the location. There could be beings from other dimensions or even never incarnated entities using the hotel portals as doorways in and out of our world. While conducting spirit radio sessions at the location I heard a voice come through that did not sound human at all, it had a robotic cadence to it's delivery. It sounded like it came straight from a science fiction movie. The message from the communicator was " WE ARE WITH HIM " the recording was done in Maddy's room. The session was conducted by researcher Ron Yacovetti and he also thinghut the voice sounded very interesting and not like usual spirit voices coming through the radio device.

The entire area has a feel to it. I talked with many of my sensitive friends and we all said you could feel the energy in the area. In some cases portals are formed by the events that happened at a location. Locations that have seen so much death will create tears into the fabric of time and space and open up pathways for travel. This can be said for hospitals and places that have battles and casualties due to the horrors of war. These openings are feared to be the way demons and dark entities can enter our reality but that's not necessarily the case. This would almost be like being at a busy terminal and watching travelers arrive and depart, some just making a stop and carrying on with their journey. Then there could be those who have something to do in the area or at the location.

SINCE THE HOTEL is used as a paranormal research location, I believe that spirits and beings from other dimensions know that this location is a great place to try and communicate with the living. The hotel almost offers nightly different research groups with state of the art devices for communication with the other side. Besides the technology that is used from the groups, many different light workers, intuitives and mediums join these research groups at the Shanley Hotel. If you were looking for a location to use or to act as a beacon from another realm this hotel would definitely get your attention. Like a lighthouse in a sea of total darkness, the Shanley calls to these weary travelers from beyond. As investigators flock and keep researching the location this is a place where two worlds meet.

spirit frequency

I LIKE to think of spirit in the form of frequency, this frequency is layered just like the depths of the ocean. When viewing the water columns, from the top you will see very clear and bright. These columns are radiant from the light of the sun, as you descend deeper into the oceans water columns, the sun's light starts to disappear and the water begins to get darker. As you reach the bottom of the water column, you are surrounded in total darkness and everything is void of light. These levels of light to darkness is where spirit energy resides once the soul leaves the body. As spirit links to the frequency of souls, it is possible that our spirit will join this frequency. There are so many layers to this ocean of light and darkness and you are not stuck forever in one level. I feel that every soul has the opportunity to improve and heal. That's what our time here on earth is all about, our souls come into our bodies to learn lessons and progress. We are spirits having a human experience. Through our time here on earth, we learn many different lessons. These lessons and our souls learning is carried into our souls consciousness. If you lived a good life and tried to do your best to help family and friends along the way, you will probably find yourself in spirit form in the higher columns of the frequency. If you were not a good person and did things that did not help or hurt people, you might find yourself in the darker frequencies. The one thing I want to stress here is that the soul is not stuck and can always learn from it's mistakes and heal. In time, spirits in the lower frequencies can ascend into the light.

At the Shanley I feel that there are so many different levels of spirits that are connected to this location. As sensitives and mediums come into this space, spirit lines there frequency with the sensitive or mediums and a connection is made. Spirit frequency can also come though radio devices and digital recorders and link for communication. Imagine that the other side is a collective consciousness, meaning spirits are interconnected and able to communicate with a vast array of other spirits in the infinite collective which transcends dimensions. This spirit connection transcends space, frequency and time. As we investigated the Shanley and spirit frequency connected with our sensitives and equipment, we received messages connected to the hotel. Through the spirit radio sessions, we obtained communication from spirit observing the appearance of some of our investigators and one even saying my name. This would make me think they are almost obersering us, as much as we are trying to contact them. From my time at the Shanley I can attest that it is certainly filled with spirit activity. I will not forget anytime soon my first experience visiting the location and interacting with it's spirits. I hope to return again in the future and document the activity, along with many other great groups of researchers that investigate the Shanley Hotel. In a way I feel that this location is almost a beacon for the living, it's frequency calling out to those researching the paranormal and giving them a place to commune with those beyond the veil. It's only been a month since I last visited the Shanley and I strongly feel the urge to return, it's that powerful of a place.

There is definitely something in the Hudson Valley that brings people together that are interested in the paranormal. One afternoon sitting in the Cup & Saucer Diner in Pine Bush, New York, I looked at the walls that are decorated with extraterrestrial art and UFO's. The diner counter offers t-shirts and some logo items, featuring the Cup and Saucer logo. Some of the locals asked where we were heading and I told them that we would be spending the night at the Shanley Hotel. I explained that we were paranormal researchers and interested in the area's paranormal phenomena. It was at that moment, they seemed all to have stories to share from strange lights in the sky to ghosts and noises that emanated from underneath the ground. After collecting a bunch of stories and letting the locals recount some interesting tales it was time to get driving to Shanley. One thing I can never get tired of in this field is how people are so passionate and want their paranormal stories to be heard. Perhaps they are seeking confirmation that they are not the only ones having these experiences, they also could be looking for some just to listen to them, when others might have turned a deaf ear. People in this field support each other and help one another tell our stories and offer a different perspective to a world people think they know.

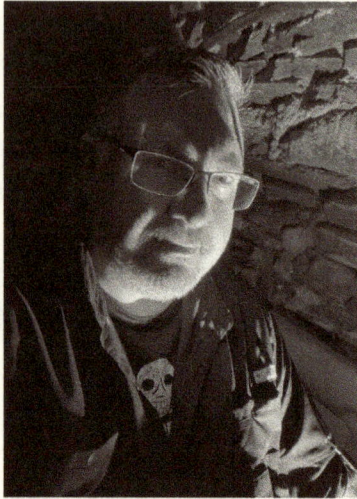

Richard Moschella in the Shanley Hotel
Basement

In my opinion paranormal phenomena are very real and it's up to the eyewitness and the researchers to keep telling our stories and making the public aware that this world is not just black and white but full of grey areas. The roads across this country are full of locations just like the Shanley Hotel, these spirits want their stories to be told and communicate with the living. We just need to listen. As a soul we are all made up of the same energy, here we are a soul incarnate, meaning in a body. Those on the otherside are souls that are discarnate, meaning without a body. We are both made up of the same soul energy. That same light shines on both sides of the veil, this is very important for those investigating locations to remember. We are connected to those on the other side and we can connect with them, we just need to learn to use our intuitive equipment. You might hear many mediums talking about before they link with the spirit they need to sit in the power. One not knowing what the medium is talking about could imagine that this must be a very hard skill to master. All what this technique is, simply is quieting your mind and connecting with the divine light. This technique will raise your vibration and spirit will lower theirs to connect with you. When connecting and sitting in the power, you will control your breathing and picture a beautiful white light growing around you. This light becomes bigger than the room you're in and can extend outside of your home and climb towards the heavens. While you're visualizing this happening, your breathing is controlled. The deep breaths in and long exhales, combined with the light visualization will open your equipment for spirit communication. I would suggest attending mediumship development classes and learning from trained professionals in the field. I have been sitting in development classes for years and always expanding my knowledge on these god given tools we are born with. While sitting in classes you will eventually get the opportunity to read for other beginners and they will get the chance to read for you.

At first, you will see that you will need to differentiate if it's coming to you or from you. If the message is coming to you, then that would be a connection from spirit. If the message is coming from you, then it is not coming from spirit but from your mind. This is very important to work on and understand. At first you might find the reading to be clunky and not make sense at all, don't worry these classes are for beginners. As the weeks go by, you will start to see your mediumship evolve and the messages coming to you will be more evidential. A simple online search will reveal classes for mediumship development in your area, Arthur Findlay College teaches spiritualism, mediumship and psychic sciences. This is a world renowned institution that many of the greats in the field of mediumship have attended. I wish you well on your journey and always remember that "A Journey of a Thousand Miles Begins with a Single Step" This Chinese proverb means that a person must begin the journey to reach their goal or destination.

Richard Moschella Spirit Art

I WANTED to add my opinions on spirit frequency and how we could try and connect to spirit at locations. The method of sitting in the power is not only for mediums and psychics, I believe that this technique can be used by all investigators to quiet your mind and like picking up a phone to make a call, letting spirit know your intentions. If this technique could be implemented not only by mediums and psychics but by investigators using spirit radio, EVP, dowsing, pendulums etc. This could become a normal practice in your arsenal in preparing yourself before you start an investigation. There are many free sitting in the power medications that you can get online and have ready on your phone. It's as simple as giving ten minutes to this method to connect yourself to spirit and soul energy. As investigators we go through many preparations to get an investigation underway, I feel that doing a meditation that could possibly make your connection to spirit stronger is extremely helpful in obtaining your evidence.

tourism and the paranormal

THERE ARE many places these days marketing haunted locations and experiences to the egear public, looking to experience what they watch on television and social media. The paranormal field is seeing a huge boom and the interest of the public is at an all time high. Paranormal conventions and events are happening across the country and bringing like minded people together. Discovery Channel has even included an entire channel on it's Discovery Plus dedicated to paranormal programming. According to a 2019 YouGov poll, 45 percent of Americans believe in supernatural beings. "Regular tourists and amateur ghost hunters want the chance to experience real magic, or what psychologists and poets refer to as a sense of enchantment," says psychologist James Houran, author of a 2020 market study on paranormal tourism. "They want to be transported out of their mundane daily lives to another place that expands their understanding of reality." I personally feel that just like in the mid 1800's with the rise of spiritualism, coinciding with the sickness and the casualties of the Civil War, we are living in another time of spiritual awakening. The public is becoming aware that this world that we once thought was black and white might have grey areas that we do not know about.

There are more devices capturing unexplained phenomena and many different platforms to share the evidence. Also just like the mid 1800's we are living in another time where death and sickness are globally in the news with the Covid pandemic that continues to take many lives. In a way, the saying "history repeats itself" is very true. I feel that this time period we're all living in is a resurgence of that spiritualist movement from long ago and instead of table tipping and spirit rappings, we have K2 meters, REM Pods, spirit radios and an entire assortment of tools to document the paranormal. Almost half of the american public believe in supernatural beings, that is a pretty amazing fact in itself. I would personally love to see that number grow and for the public to accept that the soul does survive human death and communication with the spirit world is very real. This will change the way people perceive death and let them know about the continuity of life.

I feel that places like the Shanley Hotel offer the public a chance to see that evidence for themselves, in some instances that's what a skeptic needs. They need to see the proof for themselves and have an experience with spirit. The public can book a room for the night and have the chance to experience something they would have never been able to experience. This is so important to these historical locations too, most of the money that is made is going towards the restorations to keep these locations preserved. If it wasn't for tourism, these beautiful buildings from the past would have been just that. It's through the tourism that these locations have gotten a second chance at life. It is also because of people and staff that share the passion for their history and the paranormal connection these places have. The Shanley Hotel was brought back to life by Salvatore Nicosia, in 2007 when he purchased the hotel. He was unaware of the spirits attached to the location but it did not take long before the spirits of the Shanley made themselves known to Sal. Perhaps the spirits saw the love and care that he was putting in to restore this hotel to its former glory. One could even wonder if perhaps in another time, just maybe Sal could have had a past life connection to the hotel. Maybe those who manage these locations now, might have been there in past lives and have a greater connection to them then they know. What we do know is that Sal poured his heart into the Shanley Hotel from 2007 until his death in 2016. Now under new management, the Shanley Hotel lives on honoring those that came before and letting it's guests experience the spirits that call the Shanley Hotel Home.

Shanley Hotel Seance

Spirit Radio Session

The Ghost History Medium with Ron, Lourdes and Anthony. ITC audio session.

A bullet hole in one of the door frames is untouched at the historic Shanley Hotel.

Marci and Anthony

Rich Moschella doing the estes method

NJPP Investigator Kyle with Anthony on the
third floor of the Shanley

The Team Setting Up

Basement of the Shanley

REM Pod with Photo

Objects, especially dolls can retain spirit energy
or what I like to call, spirit finger prints.

Ovilus being implemented at the Shanley Hotel

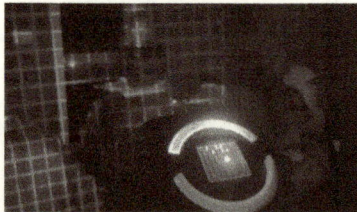

GS2 Laser Grid capturing heat and cold spots
during a mediumship session at the Shanley
Hotel

A photo of beloved former owner Salvatore
Nicosia

The Shanley Hotel's Past

Vintage Photo of the Shanley Hotel

karmic lesson

I HAD A VERY close friend that I knew since high school, he and I would have many conversations on afterlife theories and spirit communication. He had a very atheist outlook on life and felt that once you're dead it's all over. He would say just like a light going out and nothing, it's all over. We had conversations like this for years and I would recommend books for him to read and talk about many lectures and seminars I attend and he just would not open his mind to the possibility. He stood steadfast in his belief "that when you're dead you're dead". I told him that you don't have to believe every word that I'm saying but at least let yourself have the opportunity to be open to the ideas and concepts. I remember telling him about a spiritualist church that I attended and told him that they offer great programs where he could see for himself the connection to spirit we all have. I told him if you learn anything meditation would be so helpful in his life.

His life was filled with family problems and broken relationships with various women. He also was getting consumed with alcohol and getting involved with the wrong crowd. I saw him going down this darker path and did everything I could to help bring some light to this storm that was taking over his life. The only thing I could do once my attempts fell on deff ears was to put distance between us. His negative outlook and personality was really starting to get so draining to be around. I often thought of him and hoped that he would get out of the funk that he was going through. I was so happy that he found a woman that he got engaged to and we chatted briefly on the phone about it. He sounded happy and looking forward to this next part of his life. When the conversation ended he told me that he was proud of the life I made for myself and I accomplished my goals. I thanked him for the kind words and said our goodbyes. That would be the last time I talked to him, unfortunately the darkness and negativity consumed him. He was involved in a murder suicide that came to a shock to all that knew him. In the days that followed friends posted on facebook and social media memories they had of him and left words that talked about finding peace. It was such a terrible and unsettling thought to think that he would take someone's life and then his own. My heart goes out to both families affected by this terrible tragedy.

When I received information about the service they would be holding for him, I could not believe what I was reading. The memorial for him was going to be at the spiritualist church that I had told him about for years and urged him to attend. I thought to myself that it's more than just a coincidence. I remember thinking to myself how ironic that he will be in the church after all and I can only hope that you have found some peace and healing. That place that we talked about so often would be the place his memorial service was to be held at. I strongly feel that once people who are involved in acts of violence such as murders and people that have caused harm and pain to others in their time on earth, will go thogh the same life review that everyone else will go though once on the otherside. This is a time when the soul gets to see their actions on earth and learn from the positive and negative effects they had on people around them while they were incarnate. If you lived a decent life, no one is perfect, your review should take place and your soul makes the transition to the otherside. This is a time when I feel that the soul is nourished by the god force, healing and learning happens at this stage. It's also most like watching a play back of your entire time incarnate on the earth plain.

Now for those who did not live a good life and caused harm to others and were consumed with darkness, this stage of the souls' transition back to spirit could be the hell that is talked about. Imagine having to review your horrific actions that you committed all over again, these souls need more time in this stage of soul progression. This can take awhile for these souls to heal and learn from the mistakes they encountered and carried out on earth. I do however feel that they are not stuck in this place but will be able to move on once their work is complete and learned their karmic lesson. Someone that takes a life, will have to pay for what they have taken, but I don't mean there will be revenge. The soul will remain in this stage of learning and healing until it has learned the lessons it came here to learn. People who have experienced

"NDE" Near Death Experiences claim to have experienced the phenomenon describe the experience as an "extremely unpleasant from the perspective of the unhappiness they had inflicted on others, including feelings they had never dreamed of as resulting, and equally pleasant from the perspective of the good feeling they had brought to others' lives, extending to the littlest forgotten details. There is no concept of time in the world of Spirit, this time to review your life after you pass may take years. During the life review, your deceased loved ones, now in spirit can help to heal your soul as well. Spirit guides and relatives can help you along with your life review and the lessons you soul needed to learn from this experience. The life review may be helpful in the grieving process and the healing process. It can also be beneficial in the letting go process of those that are moving on to the next stage of their spiritual path and accepting the and understanding their actions and how it affected those around them.

Healing the Soul

the red veils

My Mothers NDE Experience

IT WAS the summer of 2011 and I was getting ready to go on vacation to Belgrade, Maine. I was leaving with some friends for a week-long fishing trip in the Maine wilderness. The night before the trip, I called my parents and my father informed me that my mother was not feeling well. He went on to tell me that she thought she was having a terrible chest and that she was having trouble breathing. Once I heard this I went to the drug store and purchased a few different items that would help her feel better. I dropped off the different medicines at their home and checked in with mom before I left that morning. She was sitting in her recliner and thanked me for picking up the items and assured me that she would be ok. When I got up to leave, she told me to have fun on the trip and catch a lot of fish. I would have never thought that it would be about five weeks till I got to talk with my mother again. That morning, when we were driving on the Maine turnpike, my cell phone began to ring. When I answered the phone I heard my fathers voice, I could tell by his tone that something very serious was happening. He explained to me that in the early hours of the morning he rushed my mother to the hospital and learned that she was having a major heart attack. She had major artery blockage and the doctors felt that they could repair the issue with stents being put into the blocked areas of the heart. He assured me that things were going to be ok and it seemed very routine and would call me later once this procedure was completed.

My friends and I arrived at the wilderness lodge that we would be spending the week at and it was beautiful and scenic. The smell of pine trees filled the air and a beautiful freshwater lake that mirrored the sky lay right in front of me as I sat on the dock. My thoughts drifted back to New Jersey and I could see my mother laying in the hospital bed. I knew deep down inside, I needed to get home. A few days passed with phone calls of her condition improving, not improving and then a rapid decline.On the third day of our trip to Maine, my friends and I packed our bags, loaded up the truck and headed back to New Jersey. On the way home, my phone rang and I was told that mom did not have a good chance to live in her condition. They would have to replace valves in her heart and that she is in a medically induced coma. The chances of survival for someone in fer condition would be extremely slim. Sitting in the truck and watching the road go by in the rearview mirror, my earliest memories of my mother began to play in my head. It was like watching a movie and I could not help but think about how it's all going to end. Once I arrived at the hospital, the visual site of all the tubes and machines that were keeping my mother alive was almost the site of a science fiction movie. I knew that the body in the bed I was looking at was my mothers but the vessel was vacant. It was about four weeks of seeing her in this state and going through ups and downs at the hospital. Not only having the major heart surgery performed, my mothers caught three major MRSA infections in her chest. After everything she went through, they had to remove three ribs due to the hideous infection. Finally the day came when she woke up, she was recovering and knew that it was going to be a long road in front of her. Once she could have conversations, what she started to tell me was simply profound.

Not knowing if I was ever going to hear my mothers voice again was devastating. The utter joy I felt when she began to speak and recover from her close call with death, was simply a miracle. In the weeks that followed and she began to get her strength back, she began to talk about two encounters that she had while in the medically induced coma. The first story she told me was about being in a dimly lit room and the feeling of swimming through a series of red veils. She described them to be like large hula hoops that the red veils draped over. Once she completed swimming though one, another appeared in front of her. The swimming motion continued and she went though more veils. As she told me the story, she insisted that it's probably from all the medicine they gave her. I started to explain to her that it sounds like a possible NDE to me and talked about near death experiences. To me the red veils and the hoops that she described, not to mention feeling weightless and swimming through them sounded a lot like the transition from the physical realm to the spirit realm. We are all familiar with the phrase beyond the veil. I feel that my mother got to experience the veils but did not finish the journey to the spirit realm but instead returned to her body. The story is truly amazing to me and I captured it on audio and put it on my YouTube channel. I remember talking to a chaplain that would visit my mother's bedside and the chaplain told me that reports of NDE are more common than you think in hospitals and she has heard her fair share of beautiful encounters over the years. Another NDE my mother described from her four week stay in the hospital was being in an elevator, feeling being lifted up. She described that when the doors opened she was greeted by a man wearing a white and red rope. The robe reminded her of the rope that in some painting Jesus Christ is pictured to be wearing. She felt that this man was Jesus, she did not look in his face to confirm her feeling but had a deep soul knowing that it was him. She looked at his chest and could even see the hairs that covered this area of his body. As she started to gaze up at his face to confirm to herself that it was in fact Jesus, standing in front of her. My mother described hearing a voice that said firmly do not look at his face, when hearing the voice wran her to not look at his face, she turned her gaze away. When she told me about this NDE, I explained to her it sounded to me that you were closer to physical death at this point. This would be about the time the MRSA infection had taken over her body and we were all told the chances of her survival were very little. She still wonders why the voice told her not to look at the face of the being she felt was Jesus. I could only imagine that maybe once you see the true face of God that your transition from the physical to the spirit realm is completed and there is no turning back at that point.

She still has doubts about the two experiences and at times says that it was probably all the drugs they were giving her to keep her alive. I always explain to her that those are two very profound experiences to remember so vividly to this day. They have left a lasting impression and have touched her soul and all those I have shared her story with. In my opinion I feel that she did have two very beautiful NED experiences and that her soul's journey on the earth plan is not complete yet. In the years since the heart attack she has seen me get married, grandchildren get born and enjoy not having to work as hard as she did. To me it is a pure blessing to have had all these extra years with her and watch her enjoy this phase of her life and soul's journey. When the time comes for her to make the transition from this world to the next, she already has received a tour of the other side and will be ready to swim through the veils and fulfill her soul's journey back to spirit.

a phone call to the other side

I HAVE BEEN ASKED the question "do our loved ones know, we are thinking of them" countless times and my answer to that question is a resounding yes. The story that I use to follow up this question is a personal one, my grandfather on my father's side of the family died before I was born. I remember growing up and always wondering if he would be proud of the accomplishments that I achieved, my parents often spoke of him and told my brother and I that he would have been involved in our lives. As the years went by and I visited his grave with my father, I would always have quiet conversations with him through my thoughts. Staring down at his name on the grave marker and then glancing at the grief in my fathers eyes that is still there from decades ago. I wondered if he could hear and see his family from the other side.

I was in my mid twenties when a very good friend of mine booked a reading for herself with a medium, knowing me and my interest in the paranormal she asked If I wanted to go with her to the reading. I would sit and wait for her reading to finish and also get the chance to see how a real medium worked. This would be my first time getting to see how a real medium connected with the otherside, before this time I only knew how mediums were portrayed in movies and on TV. We parked the car and started to walk up towards the mediums home, I started to feel a very intense electric feeling emanating from my shoulders down my spine. It was something I never felt before. It was so strange and came out of nowhere, I chalked it up to the excitement of seeing a medium that was going to communicate with the dead before my eyes. As we rang the doorbell, we just looked at each other in silence. To my surprise a very normal looking lady answered the door, that could have been any middle aged mother. The home had no glowing neon lights, advertising psychic readings. It was just a normal home in Paramus, New Jersey.

The medium greeted the two of us and had us come into her home, just before we sat down she looked at me and said she needed to give me a message. She went on to describe a fan that was a grandfather figure that wanted to get a message through to me. She said even though this reading is for my friends he's not letting it go and was being persistent. She described him as a big man and middle aged when he passed. She saw that he was dressed like a truck driver and wanted to recognize the junior in the family. As some family messages came through, the one that really left me in utter shock was when she told me that he wanted to let me know that he was proud of me. That connection to a question I had wondered and slightly thought in my head for years was answered in that medium's living room that night. She got everything correct, my grandfather was a very big man and was a truck driver. He died in a very unfortunate accident involving his truck, his lifeless body was discovered next to his truck on the road. The junior was a direct reference to me, I'm named after my father and the junior of the family. In no more than four minutes, my entire view on life after death changed forever. I never met my grandfather but I truly feel that night, he was next to me. My thoughts to him and questions I would ask were answered.

Now many decades later investigating the paranormal and writing about it, I always tell people that our thoughts and conversations with our loved ones are like a phone call to the other side. They don't have to be verbal, don't worry if people see you talking to yourself in your car, you can slightly put those thoughts and feelings out there. Your loved ones are only a thought way, they no longer are in physical form but are soul energy. That energy can never be destroyed or end, it's just a change from this plane of existence to the next. I have researched countless mediumship readings and spirit has come through with specific answers to questions family members have asked and even given proof it was them. My very good friend lost his mother to a long battle with cancer, they were both very into the paranormal and life after death topics. As his mother was in the last stage of her cancer diagnosis, they came up with a sign for when the son would go to a medium. His mother told him that if Bugs Bunny was mentioned in any reading he would have after she passes, that would be her confirming that the medium was in fact communicating with her. To this day many mediums that read for him are caught off guard when the image of Bugs Bunny comes into the reading. The love between incartned and discarnate souls never ends, just like the caterpillar and butterfly transforms and takes flight. It's not crazy to even have a conversation and let them know what's going on in the family, remember that our thoughts when directed towards the soul frequency are like a phone call to heaven. You can even ask for signs from spirits and when received could be a beautiful experience.

When investigating historical locations with my group the New Jersey Paranormal Project, we always like to come into a location with the names and history that is attached with the place. We start the investigation by introducing ourselves and stating our intentions and make sure the spirit knows we or there with love and respect. We ask to have a conversation and let spirit communicate their story with us. I also bring a file that to the best of my research ability has the names of the people that are associated with the location. I'll read some of the accounts of events that took place at the location and bring up the accomplishments of those from long ago. I feel that this helps make a positive connection with those on the other side, we do not start the investigation demanding spirit tell us when they died but prefer them to communicate their lives lived. We ask about life moments and events that happened that were written about, ask them how it felt to live during their time, children, marriage and then ease into the death question. This in my opinion has really helped open that communication process between us and spirit. It's just like connecting with our loved ones, by mentioning the names and accomplishments we make that phone call to spirit. Ultimately it's up to spirit if they want to communicate with you and using respect and showing them dignity shows your intentions. I feel that when we talk about their lives and the events that happened when they lived in that space, it draws the spirit close.

Establishing signs with the otherside can be a beautiful experience, as we go through our lives here on earth we can still receive signs from those on the other side. One way the spirit world prefers to communicate with the living is through symbols and signs. Symbolism can be very powerful and an easier way for the spirit to get messages across to the living. For me it's seeing cardinals, they appear in the most unlikely ways. When the day came to purpose to my fiance, I turned to my grandmother on the other side. My mental conversation went something like this "send me a cardinal when the time is right to pop the question". The day came and we went for a drive through northern New Jersey. We passed some beautiful places that offered amazing views of mountains and water. As I was driving on the highway, a truck cut me off. It is New Jersey and as Jersey drivers we are used to this event happening a lot when we drive in the Garden State. When I looked at the back window of the truck, the answer from the other side was looking back at me. On the truck's back window was a decal of the Cardinals football team. The large head of the cardinal was staring back at me and confirming my sign and letting me know it was time to pop the question.

Another way in my opinion to engage spirits to communicate is with the use of music, I have used time period music at historical and residential locations with much success.

When investigating American Revolution sites, implementing fife and drum songs and at Civil War sites using battle hymns and songs of the time period have proven to work very well in helping bridge the spirit frequency and connect our call to the other side. If you think about it, music amplifies, transcends, intensifies spiritual experiences. Most religions use music during their services to worship our descended deities and help the living connect spiritually with the higher plain. Music helps you feel your spirit and when you're in touch with your own spirit, it's easier to connect to spirit.

I like to think of spirit in the form of frequency, this frequency is layered just like the depths of the ocean. When viewing the water columns, from the top you will see very clear and bright. These columns are radiant from the light of the sun, as you descend deeper into the oceans water columns, the sun's light starts to disappear and the water begins to get darker. As you reach the bottom of the water column, you are surrounded in total darkness and everything is void of light. These levels of light to darkness is where spirit energy resides once the soul leaves the body. As spirit links to the frequency of souls, it is possible that our spirit will join this frequency. There are so many layers to this ocean of light and darkness and you are not stuck forever in one level. I feel that every soul has the opportunity to improve and heal. That's what our time here on earth is all about, our souls come into our bodies to learn lessons and progress. We are spirits having a human experience. Through our time here on earth, we learn many different lessons. These lessons and our souls learning is carried into our souls consciousness. If you lived a good life and tried to do your best to help family and friends along the way, you will probably find yourself in spirit form in the higher columns of the frequency. If you were not a good person and did things that did not help or hurt people, you might find yourself in the darker frequencies. The one thing I want to stress here is that the soul is not stuck and can always learn from it's mistakes and heal. In time, spirits in the lower frequencies can ascend into the light.

I was recently reading a fantastic book by Suzanne Gieseman called **In The Silence 365 Days of Inspiration from Spirit**. She writes, all that exists is consciousness expressed as waves of energy. You think you miss a person when they are gone, but what you are missing is their exact recipe of frequencies. Their body had a certain frequency that made you feel a certain way. Their souls vibrated in a certain way that made them recognizable to you. You cannot destroy the soul, for consciousness continues, our soul energy cannot be destroyed. We shed our human bodies but our soul, the true essence of our being goes on. The Law of Conservation of Energy states that energy can neither be created nor destroyed; energy can only be transferred or changed from one form to another. The metamorphosis of the soul from physical being to soul energy is a journey we will all experience one day. Death is very much a part of life, when our time here on the earth plan comes to an end our soul will shed its human body and go on to its next stage in the evolution of our soul.

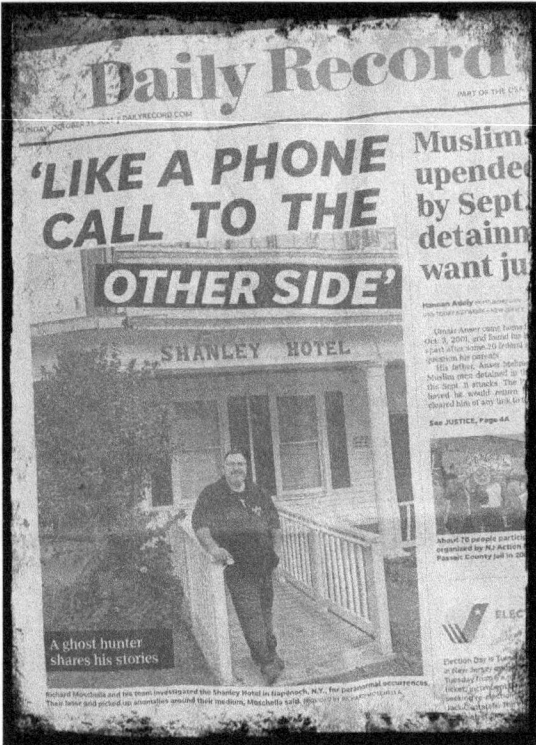

Richard Moschella on the cover of the Daily
Record - October 31st 2021

cold case and the help of spirit

I WAS SITTING in my office one afternoon and was going through my emails when the subject line of one of them jumped out at me. The email was from a very good friend of mine who is a medium and the subject of the email said two words "Cold Case". I phoned her up immediately and she explained to me that she was contacted by a woman on Facebook, the woman's husband was missing for a long period of time and after weeks of searching for him, unfortunately he was being considered a victim of foul play. My friend knows that I do spirit art and was wondering if I could try my best and try to connect with the missing man and try to get any information about that case. I explained to her that I sketch those in spirit and have never tried asking spirit to show me images of living people. This would be an interesting experience, in my development and also in my communication with spirit. My friend sent me a photo of the missing man and that was it, she provided no other information. All I knew was he was presumed deceased and that his family wanted closure on the case.

As I looked at the man's photo I closed my eyes and meditated, I raised my vibration and asked the spirit to come close. At first I began to see a map of the US appear in my mind's eye, I was being directed to move south. I saw a convenience store next to the roadside and then a wooded area just off the highway. I had the sense that the victim knew the people that were responsible for committing the crime. I wasn't sure if the victim had dementia or was intoxicated, I feel that his mindset was not clear. I did feel that two men were responsible and that they left the victim in a shallow grave. I also felt that one or both of the men probably already have records with law enforcement. Then in my mind's eye I saw what looked to be a twenty dollar bill, I had the feeling that this crime was committed over something of value but not much value.I also felt that the cause of his death was from being strangled, the image of something tightening around a neck, gave me this impression. I thought to myself what happened to this man was really so sad that this man lost his life over something so small. At this point in my communication I asked the spirit to show me who did this to him. Through my mind's eye, two people's images began to appear. One man was really thin and gaunt looking and the other was heavier and almost shaved head. I began to sketch these images, as fast as they appeared to me. Once the images were sketched and the communication was over with spirit. I sent what I received from spirit off to my friend to email to the victims family. I was surprised when I received an email back in about twenty minutes, after sending the information and sketches. The victim's family feels that the sketches match the men he was last seen with at the convenience store. The family went on to verify all the information that was conveyed by spirit. The incident happened in Louisiana and the man was missing for a significant period of time. He was last seen at a convenience store with the two suspects that I sketched. I felt that he was taken to an area that was wooded off the highway and that is where his life came to an end. The family went on to confirm that bones were found in a shallow grave and that those men that he was last seen with both have records with law enforcement. There were other images that I conveyed with the family and I shared my feelings about that being kept out of the story since at the publication of this book are part of an ongoing investigation.

My intentions for this chapter is to demonstrate how powerful spirit is and how images of living individuals were communicated by the other side. This man's spirit from the other side of the veil was able to show me the images of the men who took his life. It's truly amazing how spirit can use imagery and almost play a game of pictionary with the medium to get their message across. World renowned medium and psychic John Holland calls this your mediumship tool box. He goes on to say that spirit can access your tool box of knowledge and symbolism that is contained in your mind. When your connection is made with spirit they can access what you know and the images you associate with all things you have encountered in your life. Every medium's toolbox is unique to them, what one person associates with something could be different to someone else. For instance I was giving a reading for a friend, and all of a sudden I had the image of Superman pop into my mind's eye. Now being a pop culture geek, I am very aware of who Superman is and could not help but ask my friend is there a reason why I'm being shown Superman? He started to laugh and said that when he was little that his father would pick him up and hum the Superman theme and fly him around the house. That's an example of spirit using what we know to get their message across and make a meaningful connection.

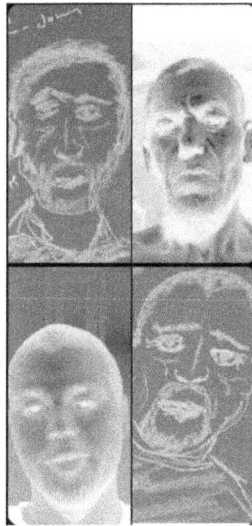

Mediumship Cold Case Art Session

As this case is currently unfolding and information being collected by authorities, I can only hope the information that I provided will help lead to the arrest of the people responsible for this crime. Spirit has reached across the veil that separates this world and the next and communicated important details about the crime that took place. These images and details came through the medium and were accepted and confirmed by the victim's family. My hope is that the people that did this will be found and the victim's family will have closure. I deeply feel that spirit just wants to be heard and for the living to know that death is not the end. In a case like this where a person is murdered, it's even more reason for the spirit to want to communcate.

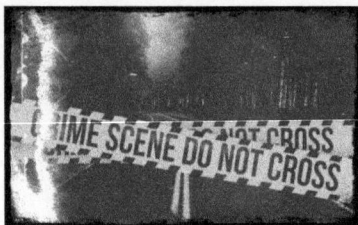

Good mediumship can help provide answers to
unsolved crimes

spirit seeker

I WAS RECENTLY INTERVIEWED for a newspaper article and the reporter asked me "why do you do this, why do you seek contact with spirits"? I paused for a moment and let the question hang there for a few seconds before I gave my response. I can tell from her silence on the other end of the phone, she was giving me her undivided attention to hear my reason. I started my response like this, have you ever stood at a memorial service, funeral palor for a loved one and looked down at your loved one in the casket or photo displayed. Their body that was once filled with so much life and the essence of what made them your loved one, you can't help but feel is gone. Now all that lies before you is their outer shell that carried that soul you loved so much. As you look at the pictures of that loved one enjoying the moments of their life, you can't help but think, is this truly the end? Where did that beautiful soul, the essence of what made this body my loved one go? Questions like, will I ever get to see and talk to them again, will come flooding into your life as you go through the stages of grief.

We have all wondered and thought about death, it's human nature to ponder what will happen to us all. No matter what, in the end we will all have to face the fact that everything comes to an end and that end is death. We all have preconceived notions of what death is from the movies we watch and ideas that were put into our heads. Some people can't even talk about death without having a panic attack and causing their pulse to quicken. In so many people, death scares and chills people to the bone. No one wants to face the conqueror known as death, so they just live their lives and do their best to not think about death until it touches them and affects their lives.

I have always wondered, is death the end? If there is life after death, what is it like? In my early ideas about the after-life and heaven, I thought we all got to hang out on clouds and listen to some rock band playing harps all day. But as I got older and interested in the topic of the paranormal, I began the research that catapulted me into the field of being a paranormal investigator. That feeling of looking down at my loved one's body that was once filled with so much life and now is devoid of that beautiful essence of that soul, we loved. I wanted to know everything I could about the process of death and the afterlife. Being a child in the early eighties shows like In Search of and unsolved mysteries presented many stories involving the afterlife fueled my passion for the paranormal. At my local library I would take out books by Hans Holzer and many notable researchers in the field of paranormal studies and life after death. In the nineties television shows like Sightings, the X-Files and Beyond Belief captivated me and made me ask more questions and turned me onto some interesting cases and pioneers in the field.

I came to find through my research and getting to know many intuitives, psychics and mediums that what we call death is a beautiful process and is just as important as birth. In death the soul leaves the physical body and goes home, no longer in pain and faced with the conditions they had in life. I came to find that my loved ones are still very much with me and are able to see importants moments that happen on the earth plane. Gifted mediums have conveyed messages that no one would have known except if they were talking with my departed loved ones. In the research of my team the New Jersey Paranormal Project, I have seen first hand at how powerful the communication with spirit truly is. I have listened to spirit radio sessions and have had spirits respond intelligently to questions I have asked. I have seen anomalies appear on camera that could not be debunked or explained. This all made me understand that death is not the end but just a transition to something else. Another destination on our soul's journey and evolution.

In recent years I have begun to open myself up for spirit communication, I have always been intuitive and have been given a loving nudge by friends that are mediums to hone my ability. At first the idea of communicating with the dead was a scary thing to me. With the help and training of some wonderful people along the way, I was guided to a wonderful mediumship training circle that meets weekly to work on mediumship development. It's been about three years for me sitting in the delpment circle and working on many aspects of mediumship. Through these classes many different topics are addressed and we learn to work with spirit and how to connect to their spirit frequency. I have even discovered my ability to sketch spirit and have begun working on spirit art. It's so fulfilling to present this form of mediumship and have the sitters' loved ones sketched and give a face to the communicators. I am constantly learning and developing my abilities. I try to read between three to five books a month on the subject and listen to many lectures and seminars. I give all the credit to spirit for my ability, I am only the channel that they communicate through and I'm honored to convey their messages. In my first book My New Jersey Paranormal Project, my fathers side of the family all displayed gifts of intuitive and mediumship. From seance's to my father walking in on his aunt talking with unseen visitors, my childhood was filled with ghost stories. In a way I feel that spirit had chosen me, maybe it chose my family. I told the reporter in my opinion I know that death is not the end and it's more like a new beginning. So when I go into locations and sit in a dark room with a digital recorder and ask countless questions, all I am trying to do is to showcase to the viewers and people that follow me the continuity of life. If in the time at the location I get only one response from spirit, I did my job as a researcher. I take great pride in the evidence I collect and messages from the spirit I convey. If I can help make people a little less scared of the word and idea of death, maybe, just maybe I did my job in conveying and showing proof that our souls go on.

I was recently talking with some friends outside a location as we began to wrap up an investigation. A group of kids passed us on the sidewalk and said wow, look they are ghost hunters. One of the kids even walked off singing the Ghost-buster theme, we all had a laugh at the interaction. I turned to my friends and said we were not really hunting the spirits but rather, Spirit Seekers. We seek them for communication, interaction, validation and contact. At times we are able to help convey a message that the spirit wants to make the living aware of or just let the living know they are still around. Death is not the end, I know that with every fiber of my being. I am honored to do this work and will always be a Spirit Seeker and if you're reading this book, you are too.

On the road and heading to an investigation at
Museum Village in Monroe, New York

before you can touch the spirit

I AM a student of mediumship and the metaphysical world, I approach the topic with great reverence and apparition for all those that have come and gone before me. That old adage "When the student is ready, the teacher appears" that truly applies to my life and probably you the reader. After all, you are almost finished completing my book entitled Spirit Seeker. It's important and vital that we never stop searching and seeking knowledge. This can also be said about our mediumship development and how we communicate with spirit. We embark on a spiritual path and especially one that brings others healing, you not only have to commune with spirit but also know yourself. Have you meditated? Do you know about energy work and balancing your chakras? Do you give time to just be still and look inward? Are you a positive or negative person? These are very important aspects for anyone to consider when wanting to connect with spirit. Renowned spiritualist medium Gordon Higginson said the following,

"Before you can touch the Spirit, you must find it within yourself. For all truth, for all knowledge and all love, must be found first within oneself. And the Spirit can never touch you, and bring love and peace within your being and from your being, until you have found it for yourself. And before you can build a picture of love from the Spirit, you must learn to find it in this life".

Spirit knows who spirit wants to communicate with, like attracts like. We need to live our lives with compassion and love. It's better to be kind than right, we need to lift up one another then tear a person down. We need to step away from an ego driven life, we are all in this life together. Wayne Dyer said it best about what ego stands for Edging God Out. When it's our time to leave this world and return to spirit, the material things that we thought meant so much to us mean nothing at death. Spirit has conveyed that the only thing that matters on the other side and what we do get to bring with us is Love and Knowledge. Just think about everything else that we consume ourselves with in a lifetime, it means nothing to spirit. When people ask if spirits care about where their body's or miss their body I tell them this. Do you miss your first car and think about it constantly? For me it was a 1993 Pontaic Grand Am and the car was great to me but unfortunately it got old, started breaking down and I knew it was time to purchase a newer car. That new car was purchased and I was then able to commute and have the peace of mind to travel long distances again. I personally feel spirit looks at our earthly bodies much like how we look at our first car or even clothes that we grew out of. Yes, it served us for a period of time but it's no longer needed. We understand that it got old and could not function or fit us anymore. That physical body had many limitations that in spirit we do not have. It helped us on our earthly journey and through the physical body had the opportunity to be a physical being on earth. A lyric of a Meat Loaf song comes to mind when talking about this aspect of our physical existence on the planet and really sums my view on the subject.

But it was long ago, and it was far away
Oh God, it seems so very far
And if life is just a highway, then the soul is just a car
Jim Steinman and Meat Loaf

Another aspect of spirit communication is understanding energy and how it impacts the world around us. There is more to our existence than our physical bodies, if you're not a reader of metaphysical studies you might find some of these concepts and opinions that I have to be far out there. Ask yourself do you believe there's more to the world than just your physical body, are we more than just beings of cells and flesh. That answer is certainly yes. How do you think souls/spirits sustain themselves? Doesn't everything take energy? If our bodies need food to produce energy, doesn't spirit need to consume something too to gain strength? Everything when you think about it costs energy and seeks it. Ghosts and Spirits are known to at times take energy from people and drain batteries before something really intense happens at a location. People at the locations have reported the sense of being drained and feeling energy depletion, this is a prime example of spirit and energy consumption. Energy can be shared and almost treated as a commodity. It's used to heal and at times provide strength through Reki and other forms of energy healing. Right now as you're holding this book in your hands, you have sacred energy residing within you. This is finding spirit within yourself and knowing oneself before you can touch spirit. You need to understand that energy connects us all and those on the other side of the veil are never truly gone. We are connected by energy; it's the essence of our soul.

Touching Spirit

David ji said in his book Sacred Powers, " The eternal flame that first ignited the entire universe burns inside of you as well. You are not just created from stardust; you also share that same devine fire that lights every star in the galaxy and that flows through every atom on this planet and cell in your body. That flame that burns inside us all, binds us and connects us to those who have gone before and those who will come in the future. This is truly timeless wisdom and gives us a glimpse of living a more soul inspired life. When you seek communion with spirit, your vessel is the most important component you have control of. To truly know spirit is to know yourself.

oh, the places you'll go

Museum Village - Monroe, New York

THE COUNTRY ROADS were fairly empty on this warm June afternoon, as I made my way from northern New Jersey to a location in Monroe, New York. As I drove past farms, country shops and even a section of the Appalachian Trail, this area was so beautiful as the sun was slowly sinking in the summer sky. The sun was going behind the mountains and illuminating the valley in a stunning golden light. Tonight's investigation would be at a location that is full of history and has a very strong connection to the past. It's places like these that honor the past and show us where we've been and how far we come. It's one thing to teach history through a text-book but to offer those curious an opportunity to walk though it, see it, hear it and touch it, it's an entirely educational experience. Museum Village was created for just that, to give those an opportunity to experience the past and almost turn back the hands of time during your visit. The museum was the vision of Roscoe William Smith. Sith was an electrical engineer, entrepreneur, philanthropist and collector who gave back to his community of Orange County, New York in many ways during his lifetime.

Smith was born in 1877 and saw so much change in his lifetime. He made his fortune as the founder of the Orange and Rockland electric company in 1905. He was very fortunate, his company was a success and his investments did very well. He was wealthy and it was the wealth that he acquired that allowed him to give back to his beloved community in many ways. One of those generous gifts from Smith to the community was Museum Village. He was extremely passionate about American history and being an avid collector of Americana. His collection of items ranged from textiles, porcelain, horse-drawn carriages, craft tools, mechanical devices and many other artifacts that he cherished from childhood. He knew these items from yesterday were slowly disappearing and wanted to preserve their history and also share them with the community.

When hard times came to local area residents, Smith would accept farm tools and artifacts as forms of payment for electricity. In 40 years Smith obtained a very large and impressive collection of artifacts. In 1940 he began to display the items and educate visitors, this also brought Smith so much joy to share stories and his artifacts of the past. Museum Village opened its doors on July 1st, 1950. Over the years young and old enjoyed visiting Musume Village, countless school trips were captivated by the artifacts and Smiths apparition for the past. On October 10th 1976, Smith passed away at a hospital in Goshen, New York at the age of 99 years old.

Those visiting Museum Village today will get to experience what previous generations came to love about the musume. It embraces its founder's vision and also honors Smith's legacy. The educational lessons and being able to experience the past is so important for future generations. This is our connection to America and our ancestors' way of life. Through educational programs, hands-on-exhibits and special events, Museum Village is dedicated to exploring and interpreting 19th-century rural life as well as inspiring an appreciation for the evolution of industry and technology in America.

I pulled off route 17M and shortly after pulled into the parking lot of Museum Village. The parking lot was bustling with attendees that purchased tickets for a paranormal investigation that was being presented by a local team. Full Moon Paranormal combines historical research, scientific data, the latest tools for spirit communication and mediumship. They go into investigations and try to capture the complete picture of the activity that is being reported. They also do their best to debunk activity before automatically assuming it's paranormal in nature. That is extremely important, especially in this field. Before you present anything that you have obtained during an investigation that you are going to label paranormal it's imperative to do your best to debunk it and try to understand how that sound, touch or visual evidence occurred.

If you are exploring all options and still can't explain it, that is when you could label it as paranormal. The ladies of Full Moon Paranormal also are believers in paraunity and feel that all groups can work together and learn from one another. This is also important to me and my work with groups, it's sharing that comradery with one another as researchers, investigators, sensitives and mediums that bring people together who share the same passion for giving spirit a voice. So much can be accomplished if we all work together as a whole, instead of independent fractions.

When I arrived I shared a spirit sketch that I did prior to arriving at Museum Village, without knowing any of the history or people attached to the location. The image of a man came to me of a well dressed man, who I associated with James Cagney looks. I'm a very visual person and I feel that spirit uses my knowledge of film and history to get their message though. It's what mediums would call their mediumship toolbox, it's our memory database that spirit can access and help steer us in the right direction during a reading. I also noted in the sketch that this gentleman is watching over the place and has a great affection for it. In the sketch I wrote the year 1950's as a significant time period for the location. I saw a visual image of the man with his arms on his side, looking out at the location. This would mean to me that he's reiterating how proud he is. I was then shown machinery and made a note of it on the sketch. I saw many children and wrote the word children on the sketch. Reminder of simpler times was a phrase that came into my mind. I saw that he could have had some cardiovascular issues around the mid 80's and then later found out that he lived to be 99 years old.

When researching photos for Musume Village and the people connected to it, this photo of Roscoe Smith really jumped out at me. It looks quite similar to the sketch that I did and some of the evendital information that I wrote on the sketch matches up to facts we know about Mr. Smith. I can however not confirm or deny it is Smith but could offer this to you the reader to view for yourself.

Richard Moschella Spirit Art Sketch of Museum Village Man

Vernon Drug Store

The first location I had the opportunity to investigate

was The Vernon Drug Store. Inside old pharmacy artifacts lined the walls and the combination of fixtures and furnishings made you feel that you stepped back into time. The 19th century drug store was originally located in Florida, NY. The original drug store was owned and operated by John C. Griddley. Then in 1883, at the age of 17, Charles Vernon became the apprentice of Griddley. In 1886, he passed the New York State Pharmacy Board exam and was given his pharmacists license. Charles Vernon became the youngest licensed pharmacist ever in New York. Unfortunately, he was considered too young, being 10 months shy of his 21st birthday, and inexperienced, not having completed the needed 3 year apprenticeship, to practice. When Griddley retired and sold the pharmacy to Vernon, New York State disregarded the age requirement and allowed him to practice. Not only was Vernon the youngest pharmacist but he also became the longest practicing one also. Vernon retired at the age of 77 years old in 1943. The Vernon Drug Store at Museum Village is a replica of the original pharmacy in Florida, New York. One could wonder if it's a replica of the pharmacy, why would spirits be attached to it? My opinion when asked this question is that a lot has to do with the artifacts that are contained behind its walls and how it's honoring that moment in time. Just walking in and viewing all the shelves with antique medical devices and medicine bottles you don't have to be sensitive to feel the energy of the building. I immediately felt the presence of an older gentleman behind the counter. I would describe him as a solid looking man with a dark handlebar mustache. I saw him wearing an white apperion over a love sleeve shirt, his thinning hair combed to the side. I felt that he was curious about what was going on in the pharmacy.

It was in the pharmacy two members of Full Moon Paranormal joined the group that I was in to conduct an experiment with motion sensors, REM Pods and a laser grid. Lisa, the founder of the group, was joined by Nicole and they welcomed our group and told everyone a little bit about the location. They placed devices throughout the pharmacy that would detect movement, temperature change and EMF changes. A laser grid was projected on the back wall of the pharmacy where activity was noted from previous investigations. It wasn't long before the group all started to experience subtle interaction with what we all believe were from spirit.

Richard Moschella with Full Moon Paranormal
Team Members Lisa and Nicole

Activity was being picked up on the pharmacy counter and this was being observed by a motion sensor ball that would go off. Also the REM Pods were picking up changes in temperature and movement. I found this interesting because the activity was occurring by the section of the counter where I saw the man in the apron. This went on during the entire time investigating the pharmacy with Lisa and Nicole, at one point we also noticed an interruption in the laser grid. For being the first location of the evening the pharmacy was really showcasing all the different tools that Full Moon Paranormal implemented here. Some of the people who were in the group reported also feeling temperature changes, while the activity was taking place. When looking at the pharmacy and seeing how all different tools were being affected by the spirit activity, this helps layer the evidence. Through the documentation and study of these places we can gain information that is vital for other researchers. Through paraunity and working with other groups you can see how activity peaks and drops, you can notice possibly if at different times it's more active than others. Through research and investigating you could find possible trigger names or items that help connect with spirit at the location. We all need to learn from one another and share our theories and ideas. There is no definitive way to investigate the paranormal, the field is made of theories and personal beliefs of investigators. I always say to people we need to be open to change and welcome ideas. We need to reserve the right to be able to even change our views from yesterday and be more informed today. The field and research is constantly changing and we all need to be prepared to educate ourselves and change with it. The ladies at Full Moon Paranormal are a great example of that sharing of knowledge and also educating the public along the way.

When investing in a place like Musume Village it's full of spirit finger prints, items that have retained energy imprints from spirit. These items were used in their daily lives and brought them great happiness or could have caused sorrow. Emotions that run the entire spectrum of human emotion, the musume even has an antique funeral hearse. Just think of all the people from the past that had once handled these objects. Then think of the land itself and its connection to the original people, the native americans. We also can't forget about the attachment that Roscoe Smith had to the property and his deep love for preserving the past. In a way if you think about it Smith also preserved a palace for the spirits connected to the past. The artifacts that line the walls in all the replica buildings and the structures themselves, this is a magnet for spirit activity. It's a place that spirit could feel at home and connected to.

After the Vernon Drug Store, I walked with the group over to the Schoolhouse where Full Moon Paranormal team members Susan and Lisa were waiting to welcome the group. They are both very intuitive and utilize mediumship during the investigation, this also helps bring forth information from spirit. Being a medium Myself I know how important it is to aid spirit and help give them a voice. The schoolhouse was dark and Susan and Lisa sat at the front of the classroom, our group all filed in and took a seat. At this location the Full Moon Paranormal team implemented a spirit radio session with the Phasmabox app. The Phasmabox software uses sound banks and also internet radio stations (optional) and embedded reverb and gives the user an (ITC) Instrumental Trans-Communication experience. This tool has been featured and used by many paranormal investigators and I have used it Myself and collected some very interesting intelligent responses.

Sitting in the schoolhouse and talking in the replica of the one room style classroom was humbling to think of what those going to school in the early 19th century would have experienced. The school house was built out of stone and children from grades 1 - 8 sat together and learned many of the same subjects that children learn today. Our school year today (with summers off) is that way because of schools like the Monroe Schoolhouse. Students spent their summer months working in the fields and at home with their parents. Then when the harvest was completed students would return to school, hence the reason school begins in September. Many boys did not graduate till they were in their upper teens. Many were pulled out of school to continue to assist their father on the farm, making them perhaps about 18 when they finished 8th grade.

Up until the Civil War, school teachers were men because they were usually better educated and were thought to be better able to discipline rowdy boys than women. But starting in the 1860s, women were chosen because they were thought to be better at caring for children, were cheaper to employ, and more readily obeyed school boards. They were required to stay single during their term. Once they did get married, they were terminated and no longer allowed to teach. Many teachers started teaching directly out of 8th grade, and were not too much older than their students. Knowing the history for a location is so important and at the schoolhouse Susan and Lisa both used historical fact to help trigger response from spirit. The group began to ask questions to the spirit that were pertaining to not being able to marry and did they feel that men were better educated than women. The phasmabox came alive with voices and they echoed throughout the schoolhouse. Being able to hear responses to questions, really amazed the group. The session in the schoolhouse was very interesting and I enjoyed the way that Susan and Lisa conducted the investigation.

Merritt Store at Museum Village

The investigation at Museum Village was coming to a close but not before all the attendees stopped at the Merritt Store. The Merritt Store was owned and operated by John Carlton Merritt from 1875 to 1924 in Marlboro, New York. This is a replica of the shop but many of the items you see inside were from the original Merritt Store. Another location at Museum Village filled with artifacts and items connected to people of the past. The connection and energy imprinted on these items is incredibly strong. It was an amazing place for Ron Yacovetti and Lourdes Gonzalez to conduct a (DRV) Direct Radio Voice session for the groups of attendees. They were joined by long time friend and investigator Anthony Simonelli from Seekers Club of the Paranormal.

Yacovetti presented a very in depth lecture on (ITC) Instrumental Trans-Communication and Direct Radio

Voice. After learning how these methods work, it was time to present the group with a DRV session. The voices that filled the room came directly out of white noise and world band radio static. This method is truly amazing and Ron Yacovetti is bringing awareness to this unique approach to communicating beyond the veil. His books Paranormally Speaking: Knowingly Talking to the Unknown and ITC Technomancy: The Magical World of Electronic Spirit Communication should be required reading for all investigators in the field.

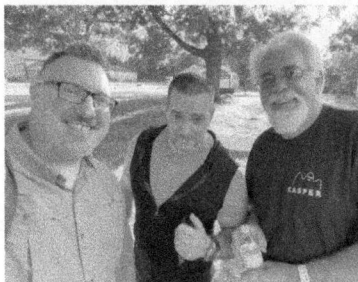

Richard Moschella - Ron Yacovetti - William Helms

Getting to investigate Museum Village with great people and sharing our passion for spirit communication made the event a great one. The ladies at Full Moon Paranormal really put together an amazing event that showcased many different techniques of spirit communication. When people find out that I'm into "ghost hunting" they have many preconceived notions from watching the countless paranormal television shows. A frequently asked question is about how much activity occurs during an investigation and is it just like the paranormal TV shows. My explanation is always the same, you can't turn on a switch for paranormal activity. The television shows that you are viewing, probably had the opportunity to film at the location that is being featured multiple days. This tremendously helps the evidence collected and gives the network enough footage they need to tell a story. There are some really amazing shows that are on television and also some not so great ones but I'm happy that we live in a time when so many shows are available and have people talking about the paranormal. Most paranormal teams that investigate locations in their state only have a single day or night to investigate and collect evidence. Once they get into the location and set up their equipment, you only have a few hours to cover the location and collect evidence. Having a game plan and communication with the team you have assembled for the event, lets you get right down to business and saves valuable investigating time. If by the end of an investigation I walk away with one solid piece of paranormal/spirit evidence I am more then happy. Yes, there are times locations are off the charts but there are also locations that are incredibly quiet. It's kind of like fishing, sometimes you use all the lures that worked last week for you but this day you're out on the water nothing works.

Museum Village at Sundown

Oh, the places you'll go when you're investigating spirit activity, I know many individuals that drive hours and spend thousands of dollars a year on travel and equipment. They spend time away from their families and even use some of their vacation time too. All for what? It's another question I'm asked when people find out that I'm a paranormal investigator. To me my observation and feeling is this: It's a fear or thought that every human walking this earth has pondered, what happens when I die? Is there something after all this? Are my loved ones who passed still around? Can they hear me? We have all been touched by the greatest thief of them all, death. Some spend their lives living in fear of death and every waking moment is full of anxiety and uneasiness when the subject of death comes up. Everyone has had an experience with greiff and the loss of someone that was close to them. Greiff in a way can act like a cancer slowly eroding the person or people that are left behind. Researching and investigating the paranormal has provided me with an entire new perspective and knowing that there is a community of life.

I have heard spirits' voices, received messages from spirits and touched spirits. I can say without a doubt in my mind that I know there is life after death. The only thing that is left behind is the physical, we are so much more than just our bodies. I think that is what brings people to the field, they seek the knowledge to help heal themselves in a way and to reach out and touch spirit. In the process of communicating with spirit you learn about yourself and the soul consciousness that connects us all. You lose the fear of death and come to understand that death is only a transition back to spirit. When you lose the fear of death, grief is an easier pill to swallow. We come to find that our loved ones are never truly gone, they are only a thought away. Continue on your journey in the field and never stop exploring, you just like me are a spirit seeker.

Richard Moschella in the The Merritt Store at
Museum Village

"The standard definition of God, "God is light," is just a simple way of saying that God is energy. Electromagnetic energy. He is not a He but an It; a field of energy that permeates the entire universe and, perhaps, feeds off the energy generated by its component parts."

— John A. Keel

about the author

Richard Moschella lives in Rockaway, New Jersey with his wife and two children. He is the team lead and founder of the New Jersey Paranormal Project. He has investigated and researched the paranormal for many years and provides lectures and seminars on paranormal topics. He is the author of three books on spirit communication and paranormal investigating. His YouTube channel features many of the locations his team NJPP investigates.

 facebook.com/richard.moschella

 twitter.com/RichMoschella22

 instagram.com/richiemoschella

also by richard moschella

My New Jersey Paranormal

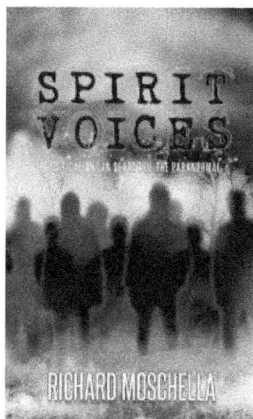

Spirit Voices: Investigations in Search of the
Paranormal

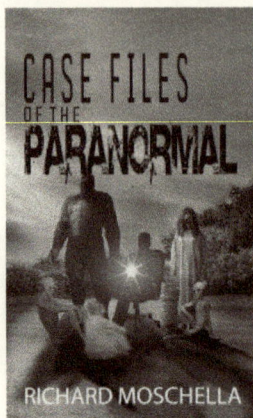

Case Files of the Paranormal

www.ingramcontent.com/pod-product-compliance
Lightning Source LLC
Chambersburg PA
CBHW022333280326
41934CB00006B/624